a sculptor's manual

Geoffrey Clarke and Stroud Cornock

a sculptor's manual

Studio Vista London
Reinhold Book Corporation New York

© Geoffrey Clarke and Stroud Cornock 1968
Designed by Gillian Greenwood
Published in Great Britain by Studio Vista Limited
Blue Star House, Highgate Hill, London N19
and in the United States of America by
Reinhold Book Corporation
a subsidiary of Chapman-Reinhold Inc.
430 Park Avenue, New York, NY 10022
Library of Congress Catalog Card Number 68–16323
Distributed in Canada by General Publishing Co. Limited
30 Lesmill Road, Don Mills, Toronto, Ontario
Set in 9D on 10 pt Univers, 1 pt leaded
Made and printed in Great Britain by
Richard Clay (The Chaucer Press), Ltd, Bungay, Suffolk

SBN 289 37020 5

Contents

CONTENTS

The modern sculptor working in the wealth of new media and processes available to him has need of an up-to-date source of readily accessible information. This manual has therefore been designed to deal with materials and processes rather than methods; thus some of the media mentioned may not (as yet) have been used by sculptors. To facilitate reference the manual has been broken down into sections each one supplemented by tables, diagrams and a list of suppliers. The text is thoroughly cross-referenced and there is an extensive glossary at the end of the book.

We are grateful to the following companies for their help and advice: Aerograph De Vilbis Ltd; B.I.P. Chemicals Ltd; British Oxygen Ltd; B.X. Plastics Ltd.

Geoffrey Clarke and Stroud Cornock

General
Each section covers a certain field and is prefaced by an introduction.

Cross-references
To avoid duplication, the reader is often referred to other sections or parts.

Buyer's guide
American sculptors are fortunate in being serviced by companies which have their research, manufacturing and distribution costs reduced by competition and the vast home market. It will be possible to buy tools and materials from local retailers, and where certain goods are high-priced or specialized, there will be local manufacturers and agents for larger firms (product-diversified companies like UniRoyal and the Minnesota Mining and Manufacturing Co.). Refer to: (a) the yellow pages in your city directory; (b) Bernard Klein's 'Guide to American Directories', which will give full details of directories covering all industries in each county of each State,—page 231; (c) your city library will have the 'Thomas Register of American Manufacturers'— 6 volumes classified by products. *British* sculptors can refer to the **Buyer's Guide** following each section, which is made practical by the small number of manufacturing suppliers. You are recommended to obtain quotations and specifications from manufacturers where there is a choice, as the small market favours price and quality specialization. Telephoned enquiries are not recommended, but written bulk orders bring discounts and carriage free terms throughout the British Isles in most cases.

Section One · PLASTER USAGE

Part 1 · Forming in Direct Plaster

Part 2 · Moulding in Plaster from Clay

Part 3 · Plaster Casting

Part 4 · Plaster Casting from Gelatine, Vinamould, Rubber
Latex Moulds, Expanded Polystyrene, etc.

Part 1 · Forming in Direct Plaster

General

Plaster is manufactured from gypsum (sulphate of calcium), baked at 205° C. As a general guide it should be understood that it is the fine white plaster (often marked 'dental') which is referred to in this text: some industrial and building grades are much coarser, and are usually coloured pink or cream. Mixed with an equal quantity of water the plaster will thicken and set within approximately twenty minutes, generating heat. Cure is achieved when the plaster is dry—the material will then have a clear ring and a dusty warmth to the hand.

Mixing

Measure into a plastic container a volume of water equal to one half the amount of plaster required. Add plaster to the water, sifting it through the fingers until it appears and remains on the surface. Leave until all the plaster is saturated and then stir thoroughly by hand (the ultimate mixing device) and disperse lumps. When working continuously in direct plaster it is often useful to retard setting: add plaster to water as usual and leave without mixing until the plaster has thickened sufficiently to allow it to be scooped out with a palette knife and worked (this will weaken the plaster).

Accelerating agents
A A thicker mix of plaster.
B Intense agitation.
C Use heated water and/or plaster.
D Ground set plaster added to mix.
E Common salt added to water prior to mix.
F Solution of potassium alum—hardens plaster slightly.
G Potassium sulphate in solution—minimizes expansion.
H Lime added to dry plaster prior to mix.

Retarding agents
A Use cold water and a thinner mix of plaster.
B Do not agitate beyond point at which lumps are dispersed.
C Solution of glue size added to water before mix.
D Citric or acetic acid about 5% to the water—e.g. urine.
E Sugar solution.
F Add plaster to water until powder remains all over surface. Leave to stand without mixing for ten minutes. Use portions with palette knife without disturbing bulk—lasts 30–40 minutes.

Forming

Some form of armature will be necessary as a skeleton over which to build up the plaster shape. This is very much a matter of invention, since the kind of shape is essentially unpredictable, and also there is the question of scale. In forming a figure in direct plaster, for instance, at half life-size, the armature could be fabricated out of $\frac{1}{2}$-inch-diameter mild steel bar through each ankle; at life-size a welded structure of mild-steel conduit piping is necessary; at twice life-size it would be necessary to use scaffolding poles. Always secure the armature to the base so that it will withstand the leverage of constant movement at the highest point. Conduit should be sunk into a makeshift box some 3 inches deep, and this then filled with plaster. The porous plaster applied to the armature will show rust at the surface, unless all metal parts are coated with a cheap bituminous paint, and absorbent materials will remove water from plaster applied and inhibit its cure—thus a framework of plaster-jointed wood should be shellacked. Anything which can be added to this framework to achieve bulk without weight will make the work less ponderous —blocks of wood, bundles of paper, etc., and over this a skin can be stretched.

For large works, or sculpture which is to be moved without being damaged, this skin can be made out of chicken wire and plaster-soaked scrim—for smaller pieces the latter will be strong enough. Scrim is obtainable in widths from $3\frac{1}{4}$ inches up to 4 feet, and increases the strength of plaster by many multiples. If the scrim is dipped in plaster and then squeezed out and hung up to dry it will form a stiff sheet with which to cover large areas.

When the armature is complete and plaster is being built up at the surface, the problem of absorption arises: wet plaster applied to dry plaster will be drained of moisture before it has had a chance to cure; it will quickly become brittle and the final work is likely to shuck off plaster in a series of layers. It is therefore essential to keep the work constantly damp—and this means a surprising amount of water.

Tools for work in direct plaster are notoriously difficult to obtain and are best forged for the purpose. If this is possible it is advisable to consider two metal spatulas and a lightweight axe head. A combination axe/adze head can be forged and tempered out of a bar of metal or a leaf spring or even an up-holsterer's hammer as described in detail in Section Three Part 4. The main problem with plaster is that it needs to be wet for building up, and bone dry for cutting away—most abrasive tools and papers clog very quickly. The best are the family of Surform Tools to remove bulk, and Wet and Dry Carborundum Paper used with water for smoothing. The latter is more effective on cured plaster.

Regular forms
In the fabrication of regular solids—such as cubes, cylinders, cones and spheres—in plaster, either for use in that material or for translation into metal, cement, plastic, etc., various devices can be used to save time. If the form is to be cast, then it is worth looking for an existing solid from which to take a mould before making one in plaster.

Templates
The following is a description of a method by which a particular regular solid could easily be fabricated, using two types of template. The example is a shape similar to that of a cigar canister, which is divided for fabrication into two shapes—a cylinder and a dome. This process is illustrated (figs. 3, 4).

A The cylindrical portion is easiest to make in two halves, using a fixed template composed of two semicircular pieces of plywood or metal. If the bulk of the implied cylindrical space between them is filled with wood or paper, and a skin of chicken wire and scrim or simply scrim placed over this bulk, wet plaster can be poured over this skin and screeded off with a bar of metal or wood riding over the templates at either end. If this is done quickly and deliberately, and the form kept wet, the resulting surface can be very accurate without much free work subsequently being necessary. As another semi-cylindrical component is needed, the templates will have been well shellacked and waxed and oiled—the first section can be removed, and the process repeated.

B The dome portion requires the incorporation of the template into the screeding tool. This is simply a matter of cutting the negative of the required shape in metal, and hinging it appropriately. It is clear from the illustration that the method is the same, but that the centrally pivoted screed now acts as a template and transfers its shape in reverse to the plaster. It would have been possible to hinge the template for the cylinder in this way, but at both ends, allowing a modulation of the shape of the screed. This is possible as the screed cannot move laterally and makes lathe-turned shapes practicable.

The three elements—two modulated on one axis and one on two axes—can now be trimmed and joined with scrim and plaster on the inside. Of course, if the final work is to be cast into another material it is unnecessary to join these plaster sections, or even to make the second cylindrical part. The shape being made, it is allowed to dry, and treated as described in Part 3.

Complex entities

This is one of those headings which implies that you should skip this bit and move on to something specific : in fact, it is precisely those problems which cannot be solved by reference to standard techniques which characterize contemporary sculpture. The term 'Construction' implies links with the Constructivist movement, and is generally used too loosely, but essentially emphasizes in its constant use the mode of invention and assembly which requires ceaseless cross-reference between materials and techniques. Plaster usage offers a uniquely flexible means of making and translating shapes, forming a basis for much sculptural activity. It is therefore useful to make some general points about the best means of using plaster :

A The strength of scrim and plaster is generally underestimated. It is quite easy to make a mould or positive surface in plaster $\frac{1}{8}$-inch thick covering an area of 6 square feet, and for such a sheet, reinforced with scrim both as a sheet and rolled into spaced ribs, to be of optimum strength and flexibility.

B There is some way of obtaining a cast of most surfaces other than liquids, casts are easily assembled, repeated and reversed. Therefore a familiarity with the idea of moving back and forth from positive former to negative mould, with any amount of assembly in between, is going to be useful.

Part 2 · Moulding in Plaster from Clay

Armature construction for working in clay is dealt with in the illustration to Section Seven, fig. 21. The considerations in moulding from a clay positive are:

A The means of removing the clay from the mould in order to replace it with the casting medium.

B The best kind of mould from which to take a cast in a particular medium.

If the clay positive is broad-based, it can be covered in plaster, the plaster and clay turned over together so that the clay can be removed from underneath, and the mould is then ready for filling. This is unlikely, and where it is necessary to disassemble the mould in pieces the first thing to decide is the order of division.

Either draw a line into the clay which implies that the form divides into two halves, or, if this is difficult, draw a series of caps through which it will later be possible to reach into the bulk of the plaster mould and remove the clay. Remember that a cylinder (a leg) should be divided just short of half-way round the form to allow one half of the mould to be pulled away. Also that at least one piece of the mould covers a sufficient area to allow the rejoining of the minor sections—a lot of small mould pieces will be impossible to stand up in one firm piece.

Metal shim—either brass or steel (which rusts)—can then be inserted into the lines drawn so that they leave $\frac{1}{4}$ inch up to $\frac{3}{4}$ inch standing proud as a neat wall. These should always project at right angles to the form and must avoid creating peninsulars. Roll a rat's tail of clay and push it over the top of this wall—this saves damage to the costly shim when excavating the mould to find the seam.

The second consideration affects the placing and depth of these seams.

Plaster: since the medium is the same for mould and cast, the mould must remain structurally weaker. Keep the seam down to $\frac{3}{4}$ inch or slightly more.

Cement and *Ciment Fondu* (aluminous cement): here the casting medium is far stronger than the mould—the seam can go up to 1 inch or more on a large cast to give maximum rigidity.

Glass fibre reinforced polyester resin: requires a very thin mould case (for fast drying), so that a standard 1-inch paintbrush can be held at 90° to the inside of the mould surface (place the seams so as to divide every form for maximum accessibility), and clean straight or curving seams for ease of excess lay-up removal.

Casting

If the mould is ultimately to be filled with plaster, the mould and cast must be differentiated—any powder colour (yellow ochre usually) can be added to the water with which the first coat of moulding plaster is to be made. Do not add more than will colour the water perceptibly, or the plaster will be weakened.

Mixing is described in Part 1.

The build-up of a plaster mould over a clay positive is best done in as few operations as possible, each successive coat of freshly mixed plaster will react with the previous coat and warp the final mould. Always make up the plaster around the seams for maximum strength to resist the prising apart of the mould parts. Slop the plaster forward with a relaxed gesture on to the clay; there is no need to change out of a dinner jacket for casting, and no need to roll up the carpet.

In theory the thickness of plaster should be equal over all parts of the mould. This may be easier if you build up one area between shims at a time.

Reinforcement

Whatever reinforcement goes on must later come off. If this means using a large chisel and heavy hammer a delicate cast within will give way. Therefore when the mould is to be filled with plaster, reinforce only with wood and iron struts attached with folded pads of plastered scrim smoothed flat on to the finished mould surface—these can be removed later before the mould is broken. For cement and *Ciment Fondu*, the mould case must be capable of withstanding tamping and carrying weight, so strengthen with sheet scrim and heavy struts. A mould to be used for F.R.P. (fibre reinforced polyester resin). Lay-up is best made by applying an even first coat followed by another coat incorporating a skin of sheet scrim to a total thickness of $\frac{1}{4}$ inch or slightly more; such a mould is flexible and can subsequently be stripped off the cast in sheets. This is practicable for plaster casting also, though only with experience. It is called a shell mould.

When the operation is completed, the plaster has had an hour or more to harden and the seams have been uncovered by scraping (this should be done while the mould is being built up, though this is often difficult), a blunt chisel can be inserted into the seams so that they may be prised apart. Pour plenty of water over the seams to reduce the suction of the clay positive. If the mould breaks or cracks do not lose the pieces, as it is simple to reassemble them later with pads of scrim.

Assemble the emptied mould as soon as possible and tie securely or dog together. It is at this stage that warping is likely to occur. Further treatment of the mould case depends on the material with which it is to be filled.

Plaster: Section One Part 3.
Cement/*Ciment Fondu.* Section Five Part 1.
Reinforced plastics: Section Four Part 1.

Part 3 · Plaster Casting

A. Casting in plaster from a plaster mould

The separating agents available are:

I Clay wash: watery clay brushed into a damp mould surface. Reliable only for small or texturally unimportant areas such as seams.

II Soda crystals : mixed with hot water to form a solution, allowed to cool, and brushed or slushed over a wet mould surface. Rinse out any crystal sediment. Useful and reliable where a heavily textured surface or one that is inaccessible must be sealed.

III Soft soap : a green jelly which tends to form a froth. Mix with cold water and brush very vigorously into a wet mould surface until a sheen appears all over. II and III allow maximum fidelity in textural registration. Fingerprints are easy.

IV Shellac, wax and rapeseed oil : shellac (french polish) is applied in two or three thin even coats at 10-minute intervals to reduce the porosity of a plaster surface to zero. The plaster should be bone dry. A separating agent can then be applied—a wax polish or a coat of thin oil (such as rapeseed). Wax will be difficult to apply to a heavily textured surface and impossible to polish. Rapeseed or another thin lubricating oil must be applied very thinly indeed, and then wiped out of the mould. If it lifts off into the wet plaster it can affect a surface. All three agents can be used for maximum security, and note that these agents obviate the need of yellow ochre in the mould plaster. Best used on regular solids and large mould parts unwieldy for wetting.

Filling

Solid
If the cast is small and may be solid, use methods II or III, join the mould parts with scrim and plaster and pour in fresh plaster while agitating. If a peg is needed for a stand, insert it while the plaster is cheesy in consistency.

Rolling
If the cast is manageable and should be hollow, use methods II or III, join the mould parts. Mix a quantity of plaster and pour into the mould. Slush and roll this around and pour out. Wait a few moments and repeat. When a thickness of plaster has been built up inside the mould, spread some scrim over the inside surface from the access point. Also some struts, if these can be inserted.

Squeezing
If the cast is complex and should be hollow, it will be necessary to fill the various mould sections before assembling them. This demands speed. All seams must be kept clear of plaster while build-up and reinforcement are effected, using scrim and wood or metal struts. When the major sections have been filled in this way, fresh plaster is run round the seams and the parts progressively squeezed and tied securely together, reaching inside where possible to apply plaster-soaked scrim across the seams. When squeezing, any seams which have been built up to 90° or more to the surface will not meet properly. The smallest caps are the last to be squeezed, and cannot be scrim-jointed on the inside. Use this method in conjunction with II, III or IV above. Where plaster is difficult to apply to an oiled surface it will be necessary to rub it over the surface with the hand, leave for a moment, and then build up.

Mould removal

The mould can be removed from the cast as soon as the cast has cooled and dried hard. A cast separated with clay, soap or soda must be chipped out, using a blunt obtuse-angled chisel and a wooden mallet, working from the top down, from the seams in. Strip any reinforcement from the mould case first. A shell mould, reinforced with sheet scrim and separated with shellac and wax and/or oil, should strip off in large flexible sections, otherwise chip out.

B. Moulding in plaster from a plaster positive

The prime consideration is the avoidance of **undercuts**—points at which positive surfaces turn away from the direction of mould removal. These must be foreseen. A piece mould has to be designed.

A simple shape could be cast by sealing it with shellac, greasing a length of cotton twine over the point of necessary separation and using this twine to cut the plaster while it is cheesy in consistency. Requires timing. Especially when this method is used to separate a mould of a part of the human anatomy.

Clay wall

When the distribution of seams has been decided (Part 2), use a roller and french chalk to make regular strips of clay and lay these across the form to enclose one section of the mould. Oil the section and cast it—rubbing plaster over the surface until it allows build-up. Remove the clay wall, make another to enclose the next section/s, clay wash the new mould section seams and so complete the cast. As this method is often used to translate a plaster positive (e.g. the screeded forms in Part 1) into F.R.P., it should be noted that the mould would in this case be very thin, the seams must be strong, excess oil must be removed and the sections can each be built up and reinforced with sheet scrim in one operation; the scrim is smeared into the first coat as it begins to go off, but must not go through to the surface. Prise the mould apart only when thoroughly hard, easy sections first. If the method is used for cement or *Ciment Fondu* the mould case may be very thick and strong.

Part 4 · Plaster Casting from Flexible Gelatine, Vinyl, Rubber Latex Moulds, Expanded Polystyrene (Styrofoam), etc.

Plaster from a gelatine mould

Gelatine moulding is described as a process in Section Six Part 1. It allows a series of casts to be made from the same mould by virtue of its flexibility, the limitation in the case of plaster casts being the repeated danger of exothermic cure softening the face of the mould. Gelatine is subject to mould (the hairy green variety) because of its organic nature—keep the mould in the plaster jacket, covered with polythene, at all times when not in direct use.

Up to twelve plaster positives can be taken from the mould.

The surface of the mould can be toughened up with a weak solution of alum; this is just like toning up the skin with alum, and the alum is brushed vigorously into the surface—dust dry with a large floppy brushload of french chalk. The surface of the gelatine can now be shellacked with two quick, thin, even coats, at 10-minute intervals. Rapeseed oil wiped on to and then off the surface effects separation; thin lubricating oil will do. It is all too easy to distort the mould surface with brush pressure and thus lift off the first or second coat of shellac. Excess oil will mix with the plaster. It is possible to take plaster casts from unprepared gelatine, though, since the gel is water-soluble, this is ill-advised.

Special hard plaster
Where a series of plaster casts are required, it is sometimes advisable to use a proprietary brand of specially hard plaster. Perform an experiment to ascertain the setting time, and the time taken for the cast to build up heat in exothermic cure. This may save irreparable damage to the gelatine later.

Method
Assemble the prepared mould within the jacket and bind or dog securely. Pour in fresh plaster and agitate the assembly by rocking and tapping to lift air bubbles. The hole which has been cut through one end of the assembly to allow this should be of a depth to allow a head of plaster.

Remove the resultant positive before heat is generated in cure—allow the mould to harden again before re-oiling and casting again. Treat any sticky or apparently damaged areas of the mould with alum.

Plaster from vinyl mould
Vinamold (U.K., various U.S. equivalents) is a patent process, outlined in Section Six Part 2. Full details are supplied by the manufacturer. Suffice to say that this synthetic moulding substance is not subject to damage by the amount of heat generated by exothermic cure, and is not attacked by bacteria or subject to hardening or shrinkage by evaporation. The mould surface requires no preparation. A hundred or more repetitions are possible. If the mould shows signs of deterioration, treat with alcohol. Note that reinforced plastic castings may be taken from vinyl resin moulds, as can cement and *Ciment Fondu* if required.

Plaster from a rubber latex mould
One of the authors was faced with the problem of making 200 repetitions of a very detailed figure. For special reasons concerning the air traps between the figure and the jacket, and the viscosity of *Vinamold*, bubbles were encountered. Gelatine was unsuitable because of the quantity required, and by experiment it was found that a Dunlop positive moulding latex would do the job. It would be necessary to consult manufacturers in the case of other specific requirements. Fundamentally, the rubber latex mould allows unlimited repetition without preparation. Due to shrinkage, the latex will not fit its jacket when baked. It may not actually need supports, so that clips at the ribbing around the seam, and some means of holding the mould inverted for filling, may well be adequate. No separating agent is necessary, the mould is proof against heat and decay. Some eruption of minerals absorbed from plaster may occur which can be removed with alcohol.

B

Plaster from expanded polystyrene (Styrofoam in U.S.)
Expanded polystyrene (X.P.) is a bulk low-density thermoplastic formed by the slight fusion of thousands of small beads (foam plastic is described in Section Four Part 3). The material allows the forming of simple shapes which might be difficult or laborious in plaster or wood, shapes which may be required in F.R.P. Such forms are expensive to fabricate in expanded polyurethane, though this is not subject to attack by the styrene monomer present with other solvents in all polyester resins and allows the by-pass of plaster processes (see Section Four Part 3). Polystyrene is subject to attack by these solvents, and it is impossible to seal the interface even with coats of paint and wax and chemical agents An intermediate translation of the shape into plaster is therefore necessary, and this is simple.

Coat the X.P. with emulsion paint twice. This will provide a basis for two or three coats of shellac to seal the surface. Then there is a choice between wax and oil to effect separation; wax will tend to fill unwanted texture, while oil will probably be quicker. Continue as under 'Casting' in Part 2. If the X.P. is removed by burning, it may congeal on the mould surface.

Plaster from wood, etc.
Clearly it is possible to arrange to take a mould from any surface—a human foot or a bronze head, a wooden form or a plastic shape—even from newspaper. It can be done by rationalizing the problem of seams, and by sealing porous surfaces before applying separating agents.

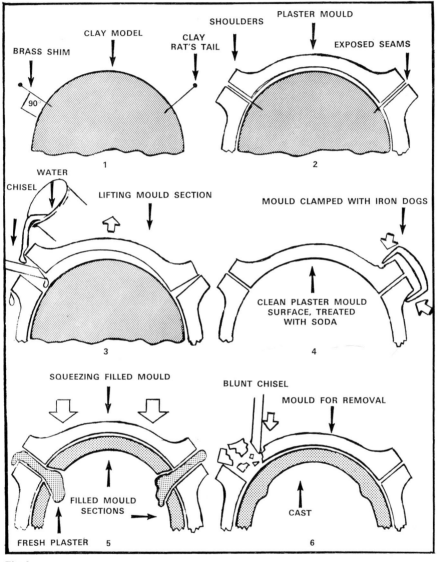

Fig 1

Sequence in plaster moulding from a clay original
In sectional form. A waste mould built up in plaster over clay, divided to allow removal of
clay by means of brass fence (shim). Strong seam shoulders support leverage when removing mould from clay (plenty of water to reduce suction). In this case the mould has been
filled in sections (leaving 5° open at seams) and fresh plaster on seams has been squeezed
out to form joint. Chip out (blunt chisel) from top, starting at seams.

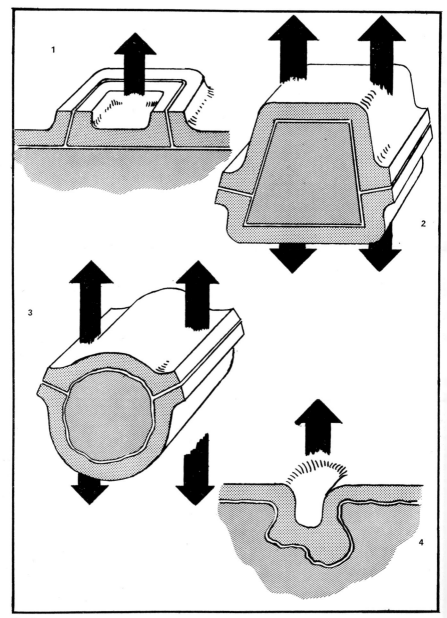

Fig 2

Undercuts: making a plaster mould from a solid or inflexible positive
When moulding from a plaster, metal or wood positive it is vital to avoid locking the mould case to the original. The solid arrows indicate the direction in which the mould sections above were to be removed, but 1 is trapped by the inward leaning seams, only the upper halves of 2 and 3 would come off, while the mould in number 4 has locked itself into a cavity in the positive.

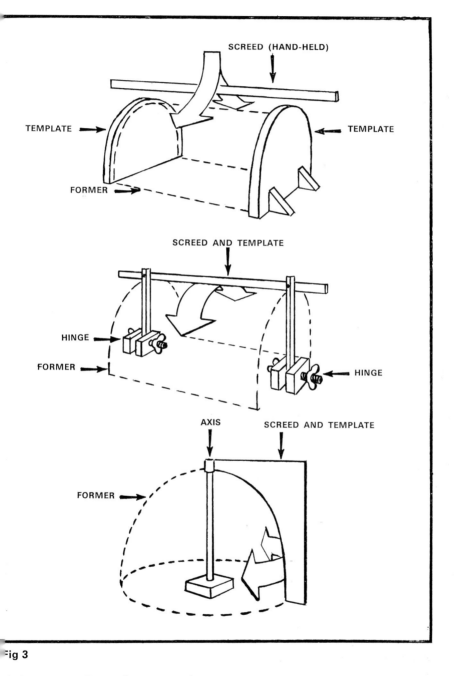

Fig 3

Various types of wet plaster screed
Note that the second and third methods would allow a varied edge to be used (almost like lathe turning), which actually occurs in the screed for the hemisphere.

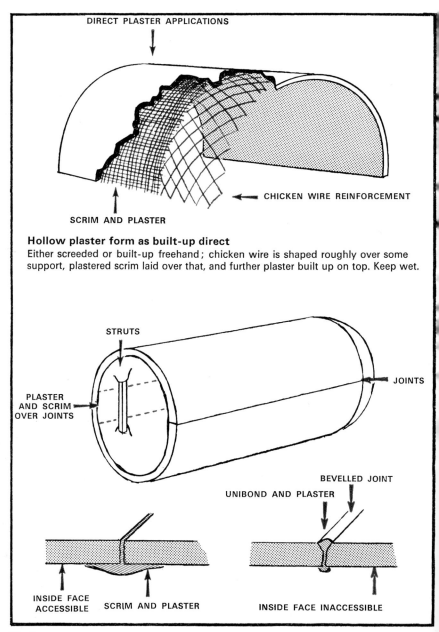

DIRECT PLASTER APPLICATIONS

CHICKEN WIRE REINFORCEMENT

SCRIM AND PLASTER

Hollow plaster form as built-up direct
Either screeded or built-up freehand; chicken wire is shaped roughly over some support, plastered scrim laid over that, and further plaster built up on top. Keep wet.

STRUTS

JOINTS

PLASTER AND SCRIM OVER JOINTS

BEVELLED JOINT

UNIBOND AND PLASTER

INSIDE FACE ACCESSIBLE   SCRIM AND PLASTER

INSIDE FACE INACCESSIBLE

Fig 4

Assembly of screeded forms
Either soak the pieces, and plaster over the inside of joints with scrim, or dry out pieces and shellac lightly before squeezing them together with plaster and Unibond adhesive. Plastered scrim can then be laid over joints in pads on inside of form. The latter method allows a cleaner job on 'industrial-finish' work and requires more care.

U.K. Buyer's Guide to Section One (U.S. readers refer to p. 8)
Unless otherwise stated, the address is London: branches in addition to London are in brackets.

Specialized sculptor's accessories
    Alec Tiranti Ltd

Armature rod and wire: Section Seven

Materials for modelling and casting

Clay and terra cotta
    Fulham Pottery & Cheavin Filter Co. Ltd

Plaster of Paris
    British Gypsum Industries Co. Ltd
    British Gypsum Ltd (Nottingham)
    Building trades suppliers
    Boots Ltd (dispensing chemists)

Scrim—jute, canvas or hessian
    E. Behrens & Co. Ltd, Dundee
    Hy. Hewetson & Co.
    Jerrard Sons & Co. Ltd, Surrey

Various Agents

Rapeseed oil
    Younghusband Stephens & Co. Ltd

Adhesive and plaster sealing agent
    Unibond Ltd, Surrey
    Building trades suppliers

Acetic acid
    Distillers Co. Ltd

Powders, e.g. yellow ochre, iron oxide, graphite powder, french chalk, various metallic powders such as bronze, gold and aluminium
    Alec Tiranti Ltd
    Lechertier Barbe Ltd
    Wolstenholme Bronze Powders, Ltd
    Metallic Paints & Powders Ltd
    Boots Ltd (dispensing chemists)

Shellac (white polish, button polish or french polish)
    A. F. Suter & Co. Ltd
    Angelo Rhodes
    Furniture trades suppliers

Part 1 · Sand-casting—the Full-Mould Process

Part 2 · The Lost-Wax Process (*Cire Perdu*)

General

More and more art colleges are now installing foundry facilities, and practical advice may be available and will probably be more accessible at such establishments than at the professional foundries, where time is money (and so is know-how).

The prime aim in all foundry procedures is to pour molten metal into a mould which is capable of dispersing heat without erupting. The most common moulding materials are therefore very porous—'grog' (a porous heat-resistant plaster) and sand. Sand presents the simplest method, since the positive pattern can simply be pressed into the sand, and then removed for replacement by metal, or alternatively a positive pattern in expanded polystyrene (Styrofoam) can be buried in sand and will vaporize when metal is poured in. The more complex process is that which calls for a wax positive to be taken from the original (via a gelatine mould), this wax form then being filled with an investment of grog, coated on the outside similarly, the wax subsequently evaporating by heat to be replaced by molten metal. The simplest and most effective method of producing cheap sizeable castings is by the X.P. or Full-Mould process, using aluminium. If it is necessary to cast a piece in bronze, some costs can be saved (given the agreement of the foundry) by doing some of the preparation yourself, for instance producing the wax positives.

Part 1 · Sand-casting—the Full-Mould Process

Various kinds of sand exist for use in the casting process. A natural clay bonded (about 4% clay) pulverized sand is used for casting aluminium, and the sand is used damp; the moisture content can be assessed by squeezing a handful. This should give a good impression of the palm of the hand—if it sticks it is too wet, and clearly if it crumbles away it is too dry.

Pass sand through an $\frac{1}{8}$ inch sieve. At this stage you have additional control over the surface texture of the casting, in that you can pass the sand to be used directly on to the surface of the pattern through a finer sieve. Perhaps the best way to gain experience of casting is to start with sand-bed and molten metal alone. Various shapes can be impressed on a level sand-bed, and undercuts can be made, for instance by pushing a metal rod into the sand at an angle. **In making these impressions it will be found necessary to make the sand coherent by tamping.** Now aluminium (preferably having a 10–13% silicon content) can be melted down and poured over the sand to form a casting which can achieve a remarkable degree of undercut for such a simply made relief.

If you now have a simple plaster pattern (e.g. a relief) without undercuts, the first step is to render it non-porous. Fill a mould box (sets of these which lock into one another can be purchased) with bonded sand, sprinkle fine loose sand over the surface to take an impression of the back of the relief. Press the relief into the sand and tamp the sand surrounding the pattern down flat. Now another mould box is fitted directly over the first. It is important that there is provision for lifting the second mould box from the first when full of sand, and for relocating it in exactly the same position again when the pattern has been removed. The second mould box is now to be filled first with fine sand to take the impression of the face of the pattern, and then with the bulk of the bonded sand, but it is clearly going to be necessary to separate the two faces of sand around the edges of the pattern from each other—a foundry supplier will provide a non-hydroscopic powder for this purpose, or a fine dry silica sand will do the same job. Tamp the sand very thoroughly so that it becomes coherent enough to carry its own weight.

Now gently remove the second mould box, filled with sand, from the first and invert to inspect the surface. When the pattern has been removed there will be impressions of both sides of the relief on view. Note that where no heavy projections exist at the surface of the relief it is not in fact necessary to take an impression of the back, and that the aluminium can simply be poured over an impression of the face of the relief and allowed to float a level back. But where the two mould boxes are being used to achieve an even thickness of metal it is necessary to decide in which attitude the whole mould is to be filled with metal, and to provide at least one feeder and one riser—though provision for more than this will be made in the mould boxes. Channels for the metal to enter the mould, and up which to rise, may be made either at the tamping stage or cut into the sand when the mould is separated to remove the pattern. **Risers must be provided at all high points.** Where the pattern has undercuts it is necessary to start piece-moulding, and an expert must be consulted.

Expanded polystyrene (Styrofoam)
X.P. for the sake of shortness—a lightweight plastic which vaporizes readily without producing too much gas in a mould. Very rigid, the material is best purchased in block form: 3 ft × 2 ft × 1 ft or larger, at a density of $1\frac{1}{4}$ lb per ft³. A pattern is made from X.P., surrounded with sand and left in the mould, where it evaporates as metal is introduced. A disadvantage exists in that each pattern is unique whereas Lost-Wax castings can be repeated up to the number of acceptable patterns obtainable from the gelatine mould and sand-castings can be repeated with the same pattern. However, the speed with which the whole Full-Mould process can be repeated greatly assists repetition. See Section Four Part 3 for notes on foaming systems.

Forming in X.P.
The pattern can be cut with hot wire, a long sharp blade or a saw. It can be shaped with radiant heat, heated metal tools, electric soldering irons, etc. Joined with a latex adhesive (e.g. 'Bostik D'), polyurethane foaming agents and adhesive tape; and smoothed with glasspaper, flour paper, wax filler.

The hot-wire cutter is illustrated in a horizontal configuration (fig. 5). Do not use an excessive amount of adhesive. Leave any soft wax to fill the surface for at least a week to harden. When making the pattern consider that the shape may well be easy to hollow and fill with core sand (to save weight), or to make in separate pieces for casting.

Foundry equipment
Furnace: A large furnace can be fired by propane gas, coal gas, or oil and a

forced draught. Small brick-lined furnaces are available quite cheaply which will accept a 10-lb crucible, which can be fired by means of a flame-gun (weed killer) running on kerosene. Place the furnace as close as possible to the pouring area, and to the kiln if Lost-Wax casting is to be attempted. Provide for the dispersion of fumes, and leave plenty of space immediately around the furnace.

Sand-box or bed : When using the Full-Mould method there has to be a bed of sand in which to bury the pattern/s for pouring, which can be anything from a swimming bath to a simple wooden box. Keep the height of the rim down to a minimum for easy pouring.

Tools: Crucible—make sure that the crucible will melt enough metal to cover your pouring needs, yet fit into your furnace. Tongs—a crucible-lifting device for use by two people. A ladle with which to stir in the flux and clean the dross off the metal, and a scraper with which to hold back the oxide film while pouring. Mention has already been made of tamping tools for preparing the moulding sand; other tools, as mentioned in the sections on Welding and Finishing will obviously be needed. A pair of tongs is useful for moving hot material in solid state.

Safety: and there is absolute need for safety clothing. A clear visor to be worn while pouring molten metal, and a pair of chrome leather gloves or mittens are essential. Wear a pair of kick-off boots or shoes with metal toe-caps, and trousers which cover the gap between sock and shoe.

Firing procedure—provide a $\frac{1}{4}$-inch layer of coke dust or a magazine in the furnace for the crucible to stand on. Gas or oil-fired furnaces should be used gently for the first five minutes, coke furnaces should be fired with Brancepeth Foundry Nuts (hot, long-burning, high-quality foundry coke, equivalent to U.S. Eastern Gas and Fuel Association size 'C') to the top of the crucible. Bring the crucible in the furnace to red heat, then fill with aluminium. A pyrometer with carbon-tipped thermocouple is used for temperature-testing of the molten metal, and may be essential for structural castings, though experience will suffice under less rigorous conditions. Up to a point, the hotter the metal the better it will run—but the hotter the metal when poured, the lower its quality when cold. Therefore structural castings should be fed with cooler metal from more feeder points.

Aluminium pouring temperatures: 650°–850° C.
A solid cube of metal is best poured at the lower temperature to minimize distortion through shrinkage. A long thin shape should be poured at the higher temperature, to reduce the likelihood of the metal cooling and congealing on its pouring run.

Flux is scattered on the surface of the molten metal in the crucible (drossing) and gently stirred in. This encourages oxide and dross to congeal on the surface, for removal with a pre-heated ladle or scraper. Molten scrap must be sprinkled with flux every time fresh metal is added. Scrape the mouth of the crucible when it has been removed from the furnace immediately before pouring. Have a hole ready in the sand for excess metal to form an ingot. During pouring further oxide will be formed, and this should be held back with the ladle or the scraper. Pursue the pouring as fast as the feeder will take the metal.

Check to see that the immediate vicinity of the furnace is free from obstacles. The urgency of pouring molten metal can turn to crisis where a man has been tripped. Metals at high temperatures coming into contact with damp surfaces will splash with unpredictable force. Coat ladles and other iron to be brought into contact with molten metal with a refractory wash. Spread sand on a concrete floor. Pre-heat ladles and tools. Use face shields, gloves and kick-off foot-wear.

The Full-Mould process: packing the X.P. pattern in the sand-bed
Having produced a sculpture as a pattern or series of patterns (for joining by welding or bolting later) it must be decided what is the best attitude in which to bury them in the sand and what type of feeding system through which to pour the metal. Feeders, gates, etc., are simple X.P. blocks set into the sand up against the pattern and stuck on with adhesive. Lastly there must be provided at least one riser or risers, ending well above the level of the pattern, and the surrounding sand can later be pierced with a pointed welding rod to vent fumes. When doing all this remember that you can only pour as much metal at one time as you can get into the crucible, and this must fill the feeders as well as the risers and pattern.

Top feed (top gate)
This is the simplest method, where the feed is connected directly to the top of the pattern, and usually quite successful. Shrinkage takes place at the farthest point and draws from the hotter metal above and nearest the feed. With a top gate this is directly counteracted by topping up. The chief snag is wash, the flow and weight of the metal damaging the moulding sand.

Bottom feed (bottom gate)
This avoids wash and turbulence: the mould is gently filled through a bent X.P. feeder which leads down to the bottom of the pattern before joining on. It is possible that the bottom of the casting may shrink on large castings, the feed system being too long for topping up. The solution is to provide blind feeders in what are likely to be the hottest (bulkiest) areas of the cast.

Dry sand-casting
Clean, dry sand, without clay or resin bonding is poured over X.P. pattern. Bottom feed to pattern is essential and a nylon core vent should rise about 1 inch away from and parallel to large vertical surfaces, to minimize hot vapour causing premature collapse. Blind feeders are the only way of topping up.

Part 2 · The Lost-Wax Process (*Cire Perdu*)

The Charioteer of Delphi—when he was complete with horses, chariot and reins—was a magnificent tribute to the technical skill of the Greek foundrymen. There was clearly no subordination of the complexity of the artist's demands to the exigencies of the Lost-Wax method, nor did he aim simply to exploit the amazing skill of his craftsmen or the superficial qualities of bronze as a material. The process has changed little since the Greeks brought it to a pitch of achievement, and it is still so demanding that very few foundries exist. Their services are very costly. If you have a sculpture in clay, wax or plaster, and it is of a nature that demands faithful reproduction, there is no doubt that bronze—far denser than aluminium, cast by the Lost-Wax process— quite different from sand-casting—presents the only method of preserving the form and texture accurately.

Outline method
A form in clay must be cast into plaster (Section One Parts 2–3—use soda crystals to separate the plaster cast from the plaster mould for maximum fidelity). From this plaster positive it is then necessary to take a gelatine mould (Section Six Part 1). Often a large or complex form necessitates the division into parts of the plaster positive before gelatine moulding: saw off extended forms away from complex junctions (e.g. just down the arm from a shoulder) with a fine saw blade or cheese wire. Excavate one face of the new joint, and carve it into a roman joint. Remember that you cannot add fresh plaster unless the old has been wetted. Glasspaper this joint when dry, seal with shellac and oil, and cast a plaster joint into the cavity on to the end of the separated form. A piece of wire buried into the separated form will make an armature for the extension.

When the gelatine mould has been made and treated, it will be used first to make two or three good wax casts, and it may then be a good idea to get some plaster positive reproductions off the mould before it deteriorates. The wax positive, having a thickness which will determine the thickness of the metal, is then invested with a mixture of ground fired clay and plaster (grog— available in proprietary brands—see Buyer's Guide). Wax runners are joined to the positive, and are brought together at one end of the form—the end from which the metal will be poured. A sprue is joined to the end of the pouring runners, and the whole complex is then covered with grog in an inverted position. This grog is then strengthened with scrim or wire mesh and plaster, and the whole placed in an inverted position in a brick kiln, where it is fired. The bulk of the wax runs out (the core being supported by nails running from the outer investment to the core), the rest evaporates. Now the very fragile mould must be transferred to the sand-pit, and buried to just below the neck. Tamping must be thorough, to provide support against the weight of metal, but remember that the core is only lightly supported. The metal is then melted and poured from a crucible as Part 1. When cold, the cast can be dragged out of the pit, the investment separated from the plaster/scrim reinforcement (for re-use), and the runners cut off with an angle grinder or hacksaw. Any holes are drilled and tapped for filling with die-cut bronze rod. Tears must be re- placed from further castings from wax portions or filled by arc welding. Final cleaning is done with small chisels—chasing. The core is removed by water jets and wire probes, and the cast cleaned by immersion in dilute nitric acid. This treatment is followed by polishing or patination.

This is an extremely complex and variable method, though large works can be cast more cheaply if it is followed up to the point at which the wax has been cored—or just to the production of the wax (without runners or core)—and the result is then given to a foundry for casting. If the foundrymen produce a bad result however—it will be your fault.

Alternative procedures: short cuts exist by means of which bronze or aluminium casts can be made, though they generally lead to metal casts rather than metal reproductions. For example, a core can be modelled in grog, and then painted with wax, which can be modelled at the surface before runners are added, etc. Or forms of a section no greater than $\frac{1}{2}$ inch may be invested directly for pouring, and joined subsequently by welding, which allows the direct modelling of the wax positives. In each case the danger is that the thickness of wax will vary enough to affect the quality of the casting.

The wax

Heat a micro-crystalline wax (obtainable from foundrymen's suppliers, see Buyer's Guide) until all lumps have dispersed, and then practise brushing it on to a cold surface. It is necessary to lay the brushload on in one movement. Use a soft brush to lay the wax into the toughened gelatine mould while it is laying open in its jacket, covering the surface evenly from one end to the other; trim excess from the seams. Lumps can be smoothed out with the heated end of a metal spatula. Where the form clearly requires reinforcement, manipulate a piece of modelling wax until it can be wrought into rat's tails: these are pressed firmly on to the surface of the wax as it lays in the gelatine mould, and modelled clean. The wax must be left to harden in a cold atmosphere. Cut a hole through the jacket, gelatine and wax on both sides of a seam (an extension of the gelatine pour-hole, for instance), dog the jacket together, and heat a quantity of wax. Allow to cool until a mist appears at the surface. Pour into the mould complex until full, and wedge upright to stand for 90 seconds or so, rather less in winter and more in summer. Then invert the mould complex in a quick and positive fashion, ejecting the wax: a deposit will have been laid down, which with experience can be governed to an optimum $\frac{1}{8}$ inch. When removing wax from gelatine mould, keep fingers wet and cold. It is suggested that the cast is stood in cold water to avoid damage. The wax can now be worked on, though in some cases this is more easily done after an investment has been introduced to form the core. Trim the pour-hole and model a piece of $\frac{1}{8}$ inch wax ready to cover it after the core has been introduced. Inspect the wax to decide where any bubbles of air would be trapped as the liquid level is rising: from these points the risers will run to the top of the cast as it is orientated for pouring. Cast off a series of $\frac{1}{2}$ inch and $\frac{1}{4}$ inch dowel rods to produce a two-piece mould in shellacked plaster. This mould will provide wax rods for the runners. Risers can be made by hanging wax-dipped string. The risers and the main runner system may be added direct as illustrated (fig. 7), or it may be found simpler to fit stub-ends to the wax, apply the first coat of grog (instead of having to apply it through the screen of runners) and then fit the upward part of the runners. Use a heated spatula to melt the end of a runner against the wax positive.

The manner and order in which the runners and risers are added, the core invested and the outer investment built up, is a matter for individual cases and some foresight is necessary when considering this problem. It is probably best to invest the core first, while the wax is held in the gelatine and plaster mould/jacket complex, and the wax cap fitted then over the carved-back grog to complete the invested wax positive. The wax can then be stood on its base, or in its pouring position if this is different, and the runners built up to just above the highest point. An investment may then be built up around the runner stubs or system, the investment and runner ends trimmed off, and the runners joined with some short lengths below what will become the sprue. The sprue can be made by dipping a paper cone in wax. Now build up enough grog around the sprue cup and risers (which should be joined to the sprue cup for support) to allow the whole to be inverted. Now, when the investment is completed, there will be a flat area for standing the mould on either end.

While the cored wax is visible, place iron nails through the wax, into the core all over the form. It is these which must support the core when the wax has been melted out.

It may be worth while to mix some fine (passed through a 60-mesh sieve) grog with an excess of water, and to have some heavier grog standing by. The first grog will be as supplied by a foundry supplier—calcinated earth clay and plaster: this is later reclaimed and remixed with one part plaster to two parts reclaimed grog. The finely sieved grog mixed wet is best brushed on to the wax, and heavier grog built up on to a good key in thick layers.

Make sure that the nails are firmly in place and well covered with grog. Ensure good joints between sections of wax runner. Provide a strong thick investment over the whole form, and reinforce well: for a small job, the grog might be poured into a container of a cylindrical nature with the wax standing inside.

The plaster mould

If this is large, and with a good thickness over the runners, it may be best to leave reinforcement until the mould has been fired. Transfer the completed mould to the brick kiln, and stand on a grid or brick channel. Build up the kiln walls around the moulds and roof in with metal or asbestos sheet—**asbestos cement sheet is unsuitable as it is likely to explode under heat.** Insulate the roof with bricks. The foundry coke must be fired gently, gradually raising the temperature until the first signs of flame indicate that wax is running out and burning. The moulds must be fairly dry before firing, or else fired for a long period to ease out moisture overnight before working up the temperature by stoking. The moulds must really be baked—every trace of wax is to be evaporated before the fire may be let out and cooling begins. Cooling is a slow process. When the kiln has been dismantled around the cooled moulds, this is a good time at which to reinforce with plaster and scrim over the entire surface. Even where the investment has been strengthened with chicken wire inside, the addition of scrim will prevent crumbling. Have everything ready in the foundry before attempting to move the moulds. Transfer the moulds with elaborate care—they are fragile, and the cores are virtually unsupported. Should the core move, the whole process must be repeated. Invert the mould and cover sprue and riser holes to prevent clogging with sand or dirt. Lower into sand-pit and pack well with damp sand—vent the sand with a welding rod.

Metal pouring and melting temperatures will be found in a table at the end of this section.

Calculate the capacity of your crucible (indicated in pounds bronze as a liquid) by multiplying the weight of wax used (including runners and risers) by a factor of ten for bronze. Melt a potful and prepare a hollow in the sand to receive an ingot of excess metal.

Melting temperatures of metals and alloys

Metals	Temperature in Degrees Centigrade
Aluminium (Pure)	660°
Cerro-base	124°
Copper (Neutral Flux)	1,083°
Gold	1,063°
Iron	1,530°
Lead	327°
Silver	960°
Tin	232°
Zinc	419°
Alloys	
Aluminium Alloy (L.M.6.)	580°C
Bronze 88/10/2 (88% copper, 10% tin, 2% zinc)	982°C

Pouring temperatures anything from 30° C to 200° C above melting points.

Foundry costing

Aluminium ingots (L.M.6)	2/– per lb approx.
Sand-cast (similiar simple shape)	6/– to 8/– per lb
Bronze ingots	6/– per lb approx.
Sand-cast (similar simple shape, bronze)	9/– per lb approx.
Lost-Wax cast (similar simple shape)	£2 per lb approx.

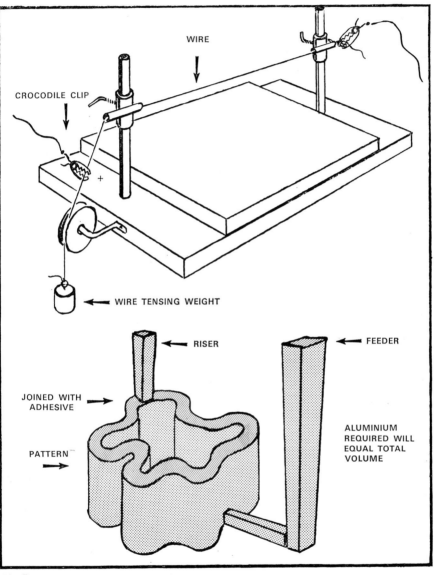

WIRE

CROCODILE CLIP

+

WIRE TENSING WEIGHT

RISER

FEEDER

JOINED WITH
ADHESIVE

ALUMINIUM
REQUIRED WILL
EQUAL TOTAL
VOLUME

PATTERN

Fig 5

Hot wire-cutting table and simple X.P. pattern ready to cast
The 24 S.W.G. nichrome wire is tensed between two adjustable supports and is connected
via crocodile clips to a mains transformer with 240 V primary and 36 V secondary windings.
In vertical form the wire hangs through a hole in the centre of the table. By moving the
positive clip along the wire the temperature and speed of the cut can be adjusted.

c

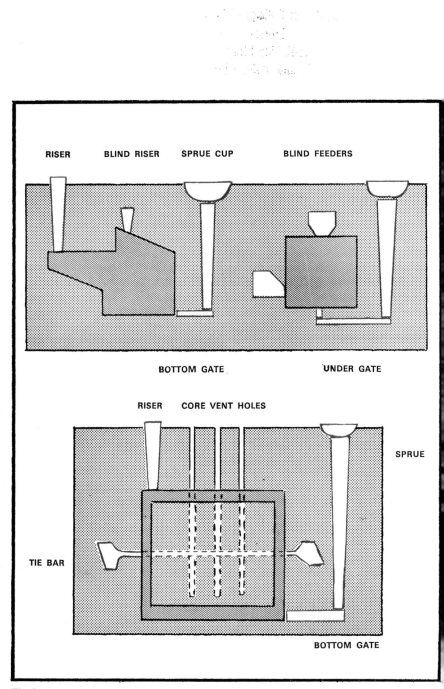

Fig 6

Full-Mould process: X.P. patterns in sand bed for pouring—sections
In each case the pattern is in black, and the various feeders, etc., in red. The tie bar is necessary to prevent floating of the core sand when casting a shape which has been made hollow.
Blind risers and feeders are necessary additions to the bulk, which assist flow of metal and
reduce shrinkage problems by creating reservoirs. Total X.P. volume is set against crucible
volume.

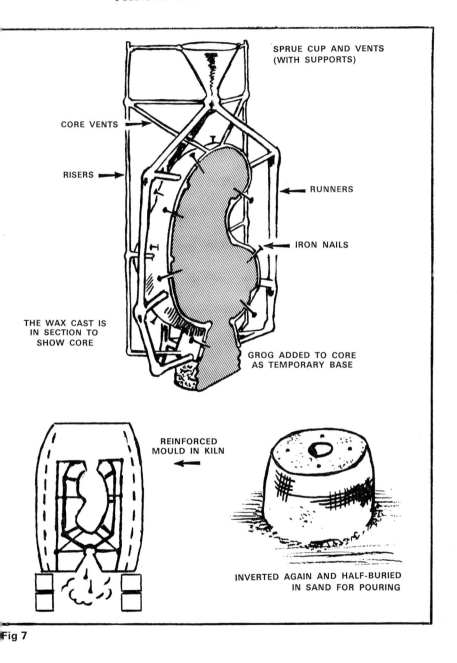

SPRUE CUP AND VENTS
(WITH SUPPORTS)

CORE VENTS

RISERS

RUNNERS

IRON NAILS

THE WAX CAST IS
IN SECTION TO
SHOW CORE

GROG ADDED TO CORE
AS TEMPORARY BASE

REINFORCED
MOULD IN KILN

INVERTED AGAIN AND HALF-BURIED
IN SAND FOR POURING

Fig 7

Lost-Wax process or *cire perdu*

A lengthy and complex process. Join all wax runners, risers, etc., with a wax knuckle by modelling with a hot spatula. Reinforce grog with chicken wire. Before removal from kiln, reinforce surface with plaster and scrim. Keep sprue clear of sand, etc.

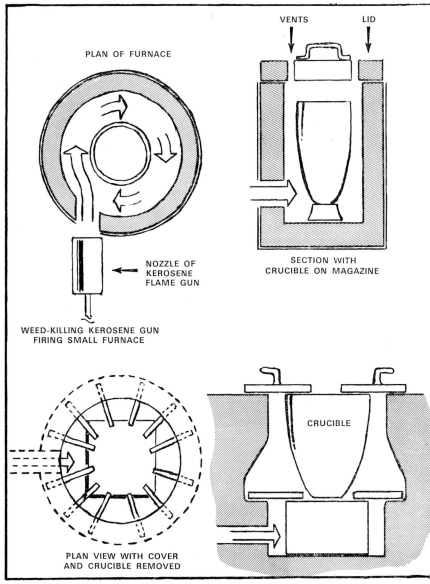

PLAN OF FURNACE

VENTS　　　　LID

NOZZLE OF
KEROSENE
FLAME GUN

SECTION WITH
CRUCIBLE ON MAGAZINE

WEED-KILLING KEROSENE GUN
FIRING SMALL FURNACE

CRUCIBLE

PLAN VIEW WITH COVER
AND CRUCIBLE REMOVED

Fig 8

A larger coke-fired furnace (below)
Buried in clay soil, fed with forced draught of air. The crucible stands on fire bricks and has a two-part vented cover. This is a very basic furnace arrangement. Note radial fire bars to support coke.

U.K. Buyer's Guide to Section Two (U.S. readers refer to p. 8)
Unless otherwise stated, address is London: branches in addition to London are in brackets.

Lost-Wax process

Foundrymen to sculptors
      Fiorini & Carney
      Fitzroy Art Foundry Ltd
      Aluminium Bronze Casting Co. (Balham) Ltd

Beeswax: soft and hard, modelling and casting waxes
      A. F. Suter & Co. Ltd
      Pooth, Hille & Co. Ltd
      Wilkins Campbell & Co. Ltd, Middlesex

Grog
      Potclays Ltd, Stoke-on-Trent

Full-Mould Process

Foundry grade expanded polystyrene
      Metalaids Ltd, Worcester

Polyurethane foam systems
      Baxendon Chemical Co., Lancashire. 'Clocel'

Adhesive
      B.B. Chemical Co., Leicester. 'Bostik D'

Investment wax
      Hooker Foundry Supplies, Brightlingsea, Essex

Hot wire cutting equipment
      Jameson Equipment (Trading) Ltd. 'Styrograph'

General foundry equiment

Foundry sands
      Associated Sands & Minerals Ltd, Suffolk
      British Industrial Sand Ltd, Surrey
      Mansfield Standard Sand Co., Notts.
      William Jacks & Co. (Glasgow, Birmingham)

Sodium silicate core sand binder, break down additive, refractory wash, fluxes and degassers, exothermic compounds, metallic sodium
      Foseco (F.S.) Ltd, Staffordshire
      William Jacks & Co. (Glasgow, Birmingham)

Crucibles and furnaces
      Morganite Thermal Designers Ltd (Worcester)

Pyrometers
        The Industrial Pyrometer Co., Birmingham

CO_2 core binding equipment and gas
        Distillers Co. Ltd

Aluminium
        Alcan Enfield Alloys Ltd
        British Aluminium Co. Ltd
        Imperial Aluminium Ltd

Bronze
        Local foundry suppliers

Gelatine and synthetic flexible moulding compounds: Section Six

Welding equipment and gasses: Section Three

Anodizing and electroplating specialists: Section Eight

Section Three · FLAME AND ELECTRIC WELDING

General

Any means of fusing metals together can fall under the heading of welding: hammering can achieve a crude weld for instance, but controlled fusion calls for controlled heat. This is easiest to obtain from a sustained electrical discharge—arc-welding. The alternative demands more skill—flame-welding— but allows more intricate handling for some loss in joint strength. Flame-welding equipment will allow adaptors to be fitted for heating, forging, tempering, cutting and so on. Electric-welding plant can be used for joining or filling holes in non-ferrous metals which is, normally difficult or impossible with flame-welding plant. Good basic flame-welding plant will cost the same as a good basic electric-welding plant, but the latter is cheaper to run.

Part 1 · Oxy-Acetylene Welding

Cylinders

Oxygen: in the U.K. pure oxygen is pumped into hollow steel cylinders at a pressure of 1,980 lb per in² at the time of writing, but pressures will soon be raised to equal U.S. standard of 2,500 lb per in² The cylinder is painted black around the collar, and has a valve at the top with a threaded collar. (Oxygen cylinders in the U.S.A. are blue or green without a black collar. Acetylene cylinders are often black or red.)

Acetylene: acetylene is pumped into a porous mass inside steel cylinders which are rather shorter and fatter than oxygen bottles. The acetylene is dissolved in acetone, which allows 400 times its own volume of acetylene to be compressed safely into the cylinder at 225 lb per in². The cylinders, which are painted maroon (red or black in U.S.A.), contain 200 cubic feet of acetylene. A valve with a reverse-thread collar is at the top of the cylinder. No change of pressures is anticipated.

Never use grease or oil on the oxygen cylinder collar. This provides potential detonation material for any spark ignition of the oxygen gas.

The present arrangement is that one of the manufacturing companies will, on a deposit or on production of trade references, rent each cylinder to a customer at a set rental. An additional fee will be charged for each separate delivery or collection of any number of any kind of cylinders.

Regulators

Single-stage regulators are fairly cheap, but are inadequate for other than brief infrequent usage, as variations in pressure within the cylinders are directly transmitted to the flame, which needs constant adjustment. Two-stage regulators carry two gauges, one showing the pressure inside the cylinder, and the other the smoothed pressure to the torch. Oxygen regulators are black (usually brass and unpainted in the U.S.A.) screw down with a right-hand thread on to the cylinder, the gauges showing, respectively, the cylinder pressure of 0—something over 2,500 lb per in², and 0–30 lb per in² or 0–70 lb per in², depending on whether the output stage is for welding only, or a welding and cutting gauge. B.O.C., the biggest company in Britain, are currently rendering all old equipment for regulating oxygen pressures obsolete by upping pressures from 1,980 to 2,500 lb per in^2 (in line with U.S. competition)—old regulators are of scrap value only; new models are the M 30 OG (0–30 lb per in^2 output pressure for welding, and cutting up to $\frac{1}{4}$-inch plate steel) and the M 70 OG (a heavier regulator for heavier cutting). Obsolete models are called 'B': B 12, and so on, and must not be used on the new lightweight cylinders being introduced now. The M 30 OG is probably the best bet for general use, though there is no difference in the prices. Acetylene regulators are marked in red. The acetylene cylinder pressure reads off on a gauge marked from 0 to something over 225 lb per in^2, and the output gauge from 0 to 15 lb per in^2 for welding and cutting. The acetylene regulator screws on to the cylinder with a left-hand thread.

Air- (gas-)lines

15-feet hoses, black for oxygen (red in the U.S.A.) and red for acetylene (green in the U.S.A.), having an internal bore of $\frac{3}{16}$ inch, fitted with connectors. The price includes the hose protectors, devices to prevent blowback through to the cylinders: any secondhand equipment should be given to a manufacturer for a checkout.

Torches and blowpipes

Here there is a choice between a shank which will accept either welding or cutting nozzles, or two shanks—one lightweight welding torch and a cutting torch. The former can be bought as a kit, e.g.,

B.O.C. 'Sapphire' Mk III, welding/cutting torch, shank/mixer, welding nozzles, cutting attachment, cutting nozzles, nozzle cleaners, spark lighter, glass-fibre case.

In the U.S.A. Sears Kit 799/T54768K2 or Oxweld Kit.

For the professional who is going to spend several hours a day flame-welding there is probably good reason to spend somewhat more and have a lighter welding torch on its own, and a separate cutting torch for steel up to $\frac{1}{2}$ inch thick, using propane nozzles (see below).

Accessories

Spindle keys, for opening the cylinder valves.
Outfit spanner, for setting up the torch.
Regulator spanner.
Welding goggles—wide-view, spectacle type and flip-up clear/opaque models are available: buy for lightness and fit.
Asbestos or chrome-leather gloves.
Ball-pene hammers, rounded at one end, one small, one heavy.
An anvil.
An openwork welded metal bench for working: this needs to be of heavy angle-iron, and to have a brick or very thick steel top.

Welding (cutting is dealt with under 'Oxy-propane', below)
A pressurized mixture of oxygen and acetylene burns at 3,500° C., and a sufficient volume of this heat will facilitate the controlled melting together of two pieces of steel to be joined and the coated steel-welding rod. Assuming a new and disassembled kit, the procedure is as follows (*U.S. readers note that identification colours are red for oxygen and green for acetylene*):

Cylinders: Roll the cylinders into the workshop: they will take a lot of dropping—but it is your risk. If they are delivered before you need them, take a spindle key and make sure they are closed off before leaving them, and don't leave them in direct sunlight. Immediately before use, open the cylinder valves and blow out any dirt that would otherwise be trapped between the gland and the regulator.

Regulators: Fit on the regulators, and tighten down the collars: clockwise for oxygen (black), anti-clockwise for acetylene (red). Couple the hoses and blow through by opening cylinder valves and turning the pressure regulator screw in until a hiss is heard. Close down.

Torch: The other end of the hoses have two hose protectors fitted, the oxygen (black hose) connect to the blowpipe connection marked 'O', the acetylene (red hose) connect to the blowpipe connection marked 'A'. Screw in the appropriate nozzle for the thickness of steel to be welded (see Table, p. 51).

Pressures: Open the cylinder valves slowly, one turn only. Now screw in the pressure regulator screws until the outlet gauges begin to register; increase to pressures as set out in the Table on p. 51.

The flame: Take the torch in the left hand and open the acetylene valve (red) on the torch: wait a few seconds until the air has blown out and then ignite with a spark lighter. Turn up the flame and adjust it down again until the sooty smoke just disappears—this adjustment is important. Turn on the oxygen control valve on the torch (black) with goggles on, and increase until there is a sharply defined inner cone of white-blue flame. This flame is illustrated in fig. 9.

Turning off: Turn off the acetylene control valve on the blowpipe, then turn off oxygen supply on the blowpipe. Leaving the pressure regulators alone, turn off the cylinder valves and open the blowpipe control valves to let out gasses in the hoses. Close valves again and unscrew pressure regulator valves. Always ensure that these pressure regulator valves are unscrewed (no pressure) before opening the cylinder valves: the gauges contain a tiny spring-like tube which will be uncoiled when gas pressure is increased (turning the arrow in the gauge), but straightened out and kinked by an immediate excess pressure.

When the neutral flame has been achieved it is advisable to allow just a slight excess of acetylene haze to surround the cone, as there is a tendency for the flame to oxidize slightly as the torch warms up.

The torch is held at an angle of 60°–70° to the work for leftward (*forehand*) welding, which is generally recommended as the simplest and most effective method. Rightward (*backhand*) welding is used only for $\frac{1}{4}$-inch plate or thicker steel, and takes some practice; here the angle of the nozzle is less (as illustrated, fig. 9). For a very strong flame weld it may be necessary to bevel the edges of the metal sheets to an included angle of 60°, but this is not the case where light gauge steel is being welded, or where normal strength (75% + for a double-sided ground-off weld) is sufficient. The hottest point in the flame is in the region immediately ahead of the cone (the cone, in fact, is hollow) where maximum combustion takes place, and this part of the flame will bring the surfaces of the sheets to be joined to cherry red heat very quickly, and they will then 'pool' and become slightly molten. The welding rod is fed in from the left at 30°–40°, in a slightly piston-like motion, so as regularly to expose the joint beyond the filler rod to the flame. The surface of the metal becomes molten, the rod is fed (not dripped) into the joint, and the torch moves on towards the left of the joint. Sideways motion of the nozzle should be kept to a minimum. When welding heavy ($\frac{3}{16}$-inch or $\frac{1}{4}$-inch plate steel) material the rightward method, which is similar to that for welding thermo-plastics, is held to be cheaper, faster and stronger: note the different angles and motions as illustrated—they are significant in achieving a good weld. If you are just learning to weld, certain stock problems will arise, mainly:

Bangs: The flame makes a subdued motor-scooter noise, or periodically cracks loudly. Increase the pressures by means of the pressure regulator screws. If you were already working at the recommended pressures for the nozzle fitted, check with the cleaners that the nozzle is free of particles, checking also that when the cylinder valve is closed and the gasses in the hoses released, the output gauges read zero (if they do not, they have been strained, and you will have to treat the reading given as 'zero', adding poundages to that figure).

Shucking: When you have finished a run of welding, knock off any excess on the surface of the metal, allow to cool, and then give the pieces some hard treatment; when you break the weld, look to see whether the joint penetrated the metal, or simply lay like glue on the surface. If the latter, make a point of watching the metal surfaces melt before moving on with the welding rod. Check that you are using a big enough nozzle. Clean the material and, if necessary, bevel to an included 60° angle.

Part 2 · Electric-Welding, Manual Electrode-Welding, Gas-Shielded Arc-Welding, T.I.G. and M.I.G.

In some respects the flame-welding process has been superseded by the introduction of cheap, portable electric-welding plants, and clearly it has been superseded in the case of the more elaborate gas-shielded arc-welding processes. All of these electric-welding processes heat and fuse metals at the point of a continuing electrical discharge across an air or inert gas gap. Advantages offered by electric-welding in general, as against flame-welding, are: intense heat—homogeneous rather than autogenous joints; instant local heat—fast working without distortion; flexibility—almost any weldable metal can be tackled.

For the sculptor's purposes, it may be said that less skill is required to achieve an effective joint using manual electrode-welding plant than is necessary for flame-welding, and less still to use the more sophisticated gas-shielded arc-welders.

Manual electrode-welding
Suited to working with: mild steel, alloy steels, stainless steels, cast iron—special problems, nickel, monel.

That list was provided by a British manufacturing firm, though it should be said that we have personal experience of arc-welding aluminium and bronze, and can say that (given the correct electrode) it works.

Plant
It is cheaper to use a welding transformer working off an A/C mains supply (single or three phase) than it is to use a D/C motor generator (however it is powered). A/C welding plant has these advantages: no moving parts—no wear; magnetic polarization, commonly resulting in 'arc blow' when using D/C is eliminated by A/C; slightly more efficient than D/C welding plant.

It suffers these disadvantages: the need to use coated electrodes; higher voltage required by A/C welding raises shock risk, should sculptor get 'in circuit'; cast iron, bronze and aluminium cannot be tackled as successfully as with D/C.

The majority of sculptors will find that an A/C transformer, air- or oil-cooled and using appropriate coated electrodes provides for immediate tacking and welding of armatures, castings, etc. For the man who spends his time in the studio working $\frac{1}{4}$-plate steel, something a bit faster, and with greater penetrative power will be necessary. A diagram at the end of this section outlines some of the points made in the text (fig. 10), and may, for instance, help to clear up questions about how A/C and D/C plant differ in practice.

Accessories
Chrome leather gloves; face shield made of reinforced plastic, fitted with lens absorbing $99\frac{1}{2}$% of infra-red and U/V rays (lens is protected with clear glass which can be replaced); electrode holder and leads will be supplied with the plant; chipping hammer to remove scale.

Free guides to the choice of electrodes are available from manufacturers.

The arc
The arc is struck when the hand-held electrode is touched on to the metal surface, to some part of which the return lead has been clamped. The electrode is withdrawn, and the current continues to flow across a now ionized air gap of up to half an inch. The arc will not jump this gap—it must be drawn from the work as the air is ionized. The bright blue arc converts electrical energy into heat (3,500°–4,000° C.) and also into dangerously strong light rays.

D/C current is polarized, and the energy exchange occurs two-thirds more strongly at the positively charged pole of the arc than at the negatively charged pole. So that, if the electrode is connected to the negative terminal of the generator, and the return lead (from the clamp) to the positive, the steel plate will take most of the heat; if these connections are simply reversed, the electrode will melt 50% faster than before, which can be useful when working on thick plate with heavily coated electrodes.

A/C current is reversing its polarity many times a second, so that heat is developed equally across the arc (U.K. 50~, U.S. 60~).

D/C plant allows variation of voltage and amperage, while it is possible only to vary the amperage of A/C transformers. It is therefore necessary to adjust the D/C plant to give 50–55 volts in order to strike an arc, whereas the A/C plant will be pre-adjusted to give a necessary 80–90 volts for striking the arc. Your set will be designed with a 'drooping characteristic', which is in effect an automatic voltage-drop, which allows you to draw the necessary 55 volts D/C or 85 volts A/C for that instant in which the arc is struck, and then draws back the voltage to 20 or 25 volts—sufficient for working (and does this quite efficiently, without wasting current in resistances). The volume of the current—the amperes available at the electrode, is decided by determining how much current will be necessary to melt the electrode. This will be indicated by the electrode manufacturer, and may range from 20 amps for a butt weld in 16-gauge steel up to 600 amps—where the electrode alone is $\frac{3}{8}$ inch thick and huge blocks of steel may be penetrated and joined. A table sets out some of the likely electrode thicknesses for use on various thicknesses of metal, but it may well be necessary to override this table in favour of that given by the electrode manufacturer.

Practice

Fit a medium coated 8 S.W.G. electrode into the holder (assuming an A/C transformer set), set a current of 150 amps, and lay a sheet of $\frac{1}{4}$-inch plate steel on the welding bench—flat. Take the electrode holder in the working hand, switch on the juice (if the neighbours object that you are dimming their lights and sending the T.V. into wild gyrations—get a choke), and then take the face-shield in the other hand. Head-shields with visors are cumbersome. Wave the shield to one side of your face and position the electrode tip about an inch above the metal surface; swing the face-shield across your eyes. You will now be temporarily blind—without the shield you would later be that way on a permanent basis. As the shield crosses your face, draw an imaginary forward circle with the electrode tip—as if describing a penny standing on edge: as the electrode touches down the arc will be struck and the motion is continued until the arc has been drawn out to somewhere around $\frac{1}{4}$ inch long (enough to prevent the electrode touching down again). If the motion is not continuous the electrode will freeze on to the sheet and it will be necessary to twist it off or switch off and cut the thing through. When the arc has been struck and drawn from the work it will become visible through the lens; raise the electrode to about 65° to the sheet and draw it slowly towards you. It is customary to practise striking the arc like this, rather than by stabbing at the metal, and to practise running a smooth bead across the face of the sheet. In industry a welder can build up $\frac{3}{8}$ inch of new metal over the surface of a casting (e.g. which is worn out) by the same means.

Observe:

> Arc blow—occurs when the D/C current magnetizes the sheet metal and pulls the arc towards the clamp on the return lead, like blowing out a candle. Change position of clamp regularly
> Spatter—occurs when the current is too high or (D/C) voltage is too high, or when the arc is too long.
> Low current—poor penetration, metal heaps up on plate with overlap, arc makes unsteady splutter.
> High current—overpenetration, flat bead, fierce crackle from arc, electrode red hot, spatter.
> Correct current—steady crackle, even slightly convex bead, stable arc which is easy to lead.

Beyond these notes the reader is referred to local welding specialists, and especially to A. C. Davies' excellent manual *Welding* (Cambridge University Press, fifth or later edition), which covers the whole subject comprehensibly without sacrificing detail as is necessary here.

Gas-shielded arc-welding, T.I.G. and M.I.G.

For the professional sculptor it is essential in any welding operation to achieve a joint which has the same properties as the base metal. Highly skilled engineers can so manage flame- and manual electrode-welding techniques as to achieve structural joints of consistent soundness, and skilled finishers have similar facility in so treating the resulting joints as to render them fit for anodizing, polishing or electroplating. But they overcome in doing so inherent weaknesses in the techniques that are an unnecessary hazard to the artist who can afford either to buy or hire M.I.G. or T.I.G. welding plant.

For a weld to be homogeneous it is necessary to fuse the two pieces of metal to be joined, or to fuse them with more of the same kind of metal, and to do this in a perfectly controlled fashion without any atmospheric contamination. Electric arc-welding allows sufficient heat to be present where it is needed to ensure penetrative fusing of the metals, but the puddle is absorbing atmospheric oxygen and nitrogen the whole time, added to which it is not always very easy to maintain a steady arc. The introduction of a shield of inert gas around the area of the weld immediately eliminates all of these problems. No flux is needed (flux causes corrosion after entrapment), no filler rod is really necessary, and the difficulties normally encountered when welding non-ferrous metals (due to contamination) are eliminated, allowing an unskilled operator to tackle almost any job with speed, ease and great efficiency. The predictable nature of gas-shielded welding has allowed the development of semi-automatic and automatic equipment.

It is possible to convert any standard A/C or D/C arc-welding plant for use with T.I.G. equipment, though it is necessary to ask the manufacturer whether he can supply a resistor (D/C: to improve low-current arc stability) or a high-frequency generator (A/C: to stabilize the alternating current) to fit the set that you have or are contemplating.

To go to the other end of the scale, there is a complete and purpose-built semi-automatic M.I.G. welding plant. This will cost considerably more though the highest figures refer to machines with purely industrial applications.

T.I.G.

As illustrated, the business end of this type of equipment comprises a non-consumable tungsten electrode around which there is a sheath issuing inert gas: hence the title 'tungsten inert gas', abbreviated to T.I.G.

Special equipment is manufactured for T.I.G. welding though, given a standard arc-welder with good low-current characteristics, it is cheaper to purchase adapting equipment. For very heavy work a water-cooling system is used to keep the temperature of the gun down, but air-cooled guns are normal for work at 200 amps or below. The sheath surrounding the tungsten electrode is a ceramic cup, the size of which relates to the recommended electrode size. The most commonly used gas in England is argon, very inert and very easily available, while in the U.S.A. there is a more readily available supply of helium gas; the term 'argon arc-welding' is therefore rather loose. T.I.G. welding is particularly recommended for use on: stainless steel, aluminium, bronze, nickel, monel, copper, mild steel (expensive relative to manual arc).

The equipment manufacturer will recommend setting up of equipment for ease and economy: this will very likely mean an air-cooled gun with two electrodes and gas cups, one for thick castings and the other for thinner sheet metal working, a hose and argon gas regulator, a cylinder of argon gas (330 cubic feet at around 2,000 lb per in^2), and lastly either an A/C or D/C smoothing device. You get hold of argon gas cylinders and refills just as described for flame-welding.

The outline method is shown in an illustration (fig. 10) at the end of this Section. Note that this is a form of welding which allows the operator to be quite delicate, and that to get the best out of the equipment the settings should follow recommendations from the manufacturers exactly, and the gun should be held as if it were a fountain pen, but passing between the first two fingers instead of just the index finger. In starting the arc, remember that with D/C current it is necessary to touch the plate, but when using A/C current the gas will sufficiently ionize the region of the weld to allow a spark to jump $\frac{1}{8}$ inch.

M.I.G.

Again as illustrated (fig. 10), the business end of the equipment is a ceramic cup producing a shield of gas, but this equipment allows the electrode to be consumed. Since, as has been said, the joint should be homogeneous, the consumable electrode must be a filler rod of the same type of material as the casting or plate to be welded, and its nature is therefore not predictable: hence the term 'metal inert gas', abbreviated to M.I.G.

In this case the whole piece of equipment must be purpose-built, and is very expensive relative to manual electrode or T.I.G. welding equipment. But the advantages offered are considerable: the operator holds a gun which has a trigger, and when he brings the electrode wire into contact with the work and pulls the trigger, the machine takes over. The direct current reverse polarity (D.C.R.P.) generator provides the striking voltage to produce the arc, and then adjusts that voltage continuously so as to maintain the arc though the operator inadvertently shortens and lengthens it, a wire feed mechanism either pushes or pulls (E.S.A.B. models pull the wire from the gun, a patent invention which eliminates birds-nests) the electrode/wire filler from a reel and feeds it to the work and the regulators provide an argon or oxy-argon or carbon dioxide gas shield. Hence the term 'semi-automatic' gas-shielded welding; note that the use of 25% CO_2 reduces spatter. It is unnecessary here to go further into a process which is covered in great detail and in widely differing terms by individual manufacturers, except to say that it is particularly suited to the welding and building up of metals in common use by sculptors: mild steel, stainless steel, aluminium, and is much the simplest available equipment to use, the fastest, the most flexible, and probably the most expensive by a factor of 300% in its simplest form.

Part 3 · Cutting—Oxy-Acetylene, Oxy-Propane, Oxy-Arc, Thermic Boring

The method for cutting is much the same for acetylene as for propane. For brevity I shall describe only propane cutting. The only differences are the pressures and the nozzles.

Propane is a rare natural gas, but a common by-product of oil-refining processes; it is cheaper per pound than acetylene, and lasts longer. It also burns at a lower temperature, so that acetylene will cut at a faster rate: this is not important except for industry.

Propane can be used for cutting steel, heating steel for bending, etc., heating the studio, thermoforming and welding plastics. So it may prove a useful gas to purchase in quantity. The order charge paid on the delivery of oxygen and acetylene will cover the propane too.

Acetylene cutting and welding regulators or cutting regulators will fit all propane cylinders and may safely be used for oxy-propane cutting.

Method
Disconnect acetylene regulator if propane is to be used, and blow out propane gland before fitting regulator (as p. 42). You will also have to get some propane cutting nozzles, which are two piece to facilitate cleaning. Oxy-acetylene and oxy-propane cutting pressures and nozzle sizes are not critical—but a Table is given on p. 52.

When metal has been raised to incandescent heat a stream of oxygen will cause combustion to take place in the metal itself. This is the cutting principle, where oxy-acetylene is used to form a neutral flame for heating, and a third stream of oxygen is used (by depressing a lever) to burn a cut in the metal.

Set the pressures with gas flowing through each pipe in turn, by opening the control on the torch and then adjusting the regulator. Ignite the acetylene and open heating oxygen valve to give a neutral flame; depress the cutting lever, and adjust again to give a neutral flame. Remove all rust and scale from scrap metal before commencing cut.

Use a length of angle iron for a guide on straight-line cutting, a clear chalk mark for curves. Start at that point farthest away from you. Leave space below the cutting line for material to be blown away. Using the heating flame, raise the edge of the plate to melting point with the torch blowpipe held vertically above it, then release the cutting oxygen with the thumb, and draw the cutter towards you. When cutting cast iron, use acetylene gas, and maintain an excess of acetylene in the flame.

Oxy-arc
Oxygen supply is fed through a gun. The 'nozzle' of which is a hollow electrode, the gun the electrode holder, the trigger controlling the oxygen supply. The arc is struck in the normal way and trigger pulled to start flow of cutting oxygen.

Thermic boring of steel and concrete
This is a cheap, fast way of drilling and cutting really heavy sections of virtually any material, such as cement, reinforced concrete, steel, iron, etc. The higher the ferrous content of the material, the faster the job.

Requirements: two or three cylinders of oxygen connected in series to a heavy-duty regulator, and from there via an oxygen hose to a metal lance-holder. This is designed to take a 'packed lance', which is a length of steel pipe containing lengths of welding rod. Pure oxygen is then passed through the packed lance and ignited. The packed lance is then shoved up against (for instance) a foot-thick slab of reinforced concrete. Packed lance is consumed at the rate of 10 feet per 1 foot reinforced concrete cut through. Packed lance is purchased in 10-feet lengths; it is cheaper than anti-tank shells, and nearly as fast.

Part 4 · Annealing, Tempering, Forging, Metal Spraying

Annealing
For all but the last of the processes described in this part, it is best to have a large diameter gas main fitted in the studio, terminating in a nozzle on to which a rubber hose for a torch can be fitted, and in a burner situated in a shallow metal tray. The latter will form a furnace; this can simply be welded up with four legs supporting a tray, over which a hood is fitted to lead fumes away. A small air pump, driven by an electric motor, will feed both torch and furnace. Taps for gas control are fitted before mains divides to nozzles, before each nozzle and at the torch for adjustment. Air taps are fitted at the torch for adjustment and at the forge. Always ignite gas before starting air pump. Fit the forge tray out with fire-bricks and a heap of foundry coke or clinker—this gives a red-hot mass into which steel can be introduced for mass heating, while the torch provides for local heating prior to bending or tempering. You cannot really call this a forge unless it is also equipped with a heavy anvil, or light one bolted down, tongs, for handling hot metal, safety clothes—visor, gauntlets, etc.—oil bath for annealing, ball-pene hammers for forging.

Either equipped as above, or with pliers and an oxy-acetylene torch, assume that it is necessary to forge an axe/adze head from an upholsterer's hammer.

D

Tempering and annealing

The hardness of a metal is precisely related to the temperature from which it lasted cooled, and the speed with which it cooled. Mild steel (it is not possible to alter the crystalline structure of cast iron) and tool steels vary in consistency, so in certain cases the following may be found difficult: if the metal contains impurities or faults it may crack when quenched at normally reasonable temperatures, and so on. To remove all temper from the metal which is to be forged, and which therefore needs to be as soft as possible, the steel is heated to a cherry red, and then allowed to cool slowly: this is termed 'annealing'.

Assuming now that the metal has been forged to shape as described later in this part, or that a stone-carving chisel is to be tempered, there is an essential preface to the final tempering of the metal. Heat the working ends of the tool one at a time to cherry red, and then plunge the heated tool into a bath of oil (linseed oil, for example). Oil is preferable to cold water for quenching, because it removes the heat of the metal slightly less violently. The metal is now so hard around the working end of the blade as to be brittle. Note: if you heat the steel beyond cherry red to white-heat, it is likely to burn and be reduced in quality.

The hardened metal can be burnished with fine emery cloth to show subsequent temper colours clearly. These temper colours are set out in the table following this section, but they remain a very approximate guide. The colours related to the temperatures to which the metal is now heated will appear in order (though some of them may be transient or difficult to distinguish), and the process can be stopped at any point (securing the hardness related to a particular temperature) by immersion in the oil bath. Their order of appearance will be from the low-temperature end of the scale: light straw, straw, dark straw, bronze, violet, dark blue and light blue. It is important here to note that you are reducing the hardness of each part of the metal as it goes through the colours from the original hardness frozen into the metal. Since the body of the blade must be resilient, while the tip keeps hard, it is necessary to place the blade over a low heat about an inch from the tip. As it heats, the temper will be removed from the body of the blade (which will colour from straw through blue), while the colours spread up to the tip. For use on very hard materials the tool can be quenched before the light straw colour has really reached the tip, and this may be satisfactory for tools which need a keen edge but will not be chipped by virtue of their brittle temper. General stonecarving tools are better reduced to a violet colour at the tip.

Forging

The annealed metal for forging may develop faults while being hammered and it is therefore necessary to clean and examine the work from time to time. Wrought iron is the easiest metal to forge, but cannot be flame-welded and will not suffer tempering. Mild steel hexagonal bar is normally used for forging metal spatulas, while an upholsterer's hammer or a piece of leaf spring will make a useful axe. Sheet metal can be dished by cold hammering over a wooden block. But the bulk of forging work consists of heating a piece of metal to a cherry red (no further, or it will 'burn'), transferring it quickly to a heavy anvil, or a small one secured to a block, where it can be pushed and drawn into shape with a heavy hammer.

Do one thing at a time: draw a body of metal out by hammering it in one plane, then turn sideways and shape it, introducing bends at a later stage. Where the metal has not been properly annealed, or where it has been hammered cold, or even where it has simply been hammered too thin, it may show signs of splitting into small feathers of steel. These can all be ground off later and the whole piece cut into shape with files. The only real limitation on forging is that there is enough metal there to move with the hammer. Sculptors like Bryan Kneale have developed the use of forging to the point at which its rather folksy flavour has been lost, and the steel becomes a plastic substance.

Metal spraying

Two methods of spraying exist, which use either powdered or wire-formed metals to atomize and project on to surfaces, and it is possible in fact to spray other non-metallic substances, including ceramics. Some firms claim to have perfected technique to the point at which they are able to coat textiles with metals. The material to be sprayed must first be shot-blasted in most cases, though this is not necessary where a good key is already present in the texture of the sculpture material—for instance, plaster may be sprayed direct with metal. For maximum protection the wire-spray method is probably superior to the powder system.

Leftward flame welding

Steel plate (inch)	Preparation	Rod (inch)	Blowpipe	Oxy (lb/in²)	Acet (lb/in²)
$\frac{1}{16}$	Butt joint, edges turned up at 90° $\frac{1}{8}$ inch	—	2–3	2	3
$\frac{1}{8}$	$\frac{1}{16}$ inch gap	$\frac{3}{32}$	7	2	3
$\frac{3}{16}$	70° vee joint	$\frac{1}{8}$	13	3	3
$\frac{1}{4}$	90° vee joint	$\frac{1}{8}$	18	3	4

Rightward flame welding

Steel plate (inch)	Preparation	Rod (inch)	Blowpipe	Oxy (lb/in²)	Acet (lb/in²)
$\frac{1}{4}$	$\frac{1}{8}$ inch gap	$\frac{1}{8}$	18	3	4
$\frac{3}{8}$	60° vee joint, $\frac{1}{8}$ inch gap	$\frac{3}{16}$	35	4	5
1	Double 60° vee, $\frac{1}{8}$ inch gap	$\frac{1}{4}$	70	6	10

Electric welding

Steel plate (inch)	Preparation	Electrode size (S.W.G.)	No. of runs
$\frac{1}{16}$	Butt	14	1
$\frac{1}{8}$	$\frac{1}{16}$ inch gap	12	1
$\frac{3}{16}$	$\frac{1}{8}$ inch gap	10	1
$\frac{1}{4}$	$\frac{1}{8}$ inch gap	8	1
$\frac{1}{2}$	60° vee, $\frac{1}{8}$ inch gap	10, 8, 6	3
1	Double 60° vee, $\frac{1}{16}$ inch gap	8, 6, 4	3

Electrode sizes and general reference for standard wire gauges

S.W.G.	Diameter (approximate)
4	$\frac{1}{4}$ (inch)
6	$\frac{3}{16}$
8	$\frac{5}{32}$
10	$\frac{1}{8}$
12	$\frac{3}{32}$
14	$\frac{5}{64}$

Tempering of steel (approx. guide). Temperature in Degrees Centigrade

Temperature		Colour	
	220°		Pale yellow (hard)
	240°		Straw
	260°		Light brown
	270°		Bronze
	280°		Purple
	290°		Blue
	300°		Dark blue (soft)

Gas cylinder identification chart. British Standard Specification

Chem. symbol	Gas	Inflammable/ non-inflammable	Colour/marking	Regulator thread
O	Oxygen	Non	Black	Clockwise
C_2H_2	Acetylene	Inf	Maroon	Counter
—	Coal gas	Inf	Red, 'Coal Gas'	Counter
H	Hydrogen	Inf	Red	Counter
N	Nitrogen	Non	Grey, black band	Clockwise
—	Air	Non	Grey	Clockwise
C_3H_6	Propane	Inf	Red, 'Propane'	Counter
A	Argon	Non	Blue	Clockwise
He	Helium	Non	Medium brown	Clockwise
CO_2	Carbon-Dioxide	Non	Black	Clockwise

Flame cutting: acetylene or propane and oxygen

Steel plate (inch)	Oxygen (lb/in²)	Acetylene (lb/in²)	Nozzle (inch)
Up to $\frac{1}{4}$	25	2	$\frac{1}{32}$
Up to $\frac{1}{2}$	30	2	$\frac{3}{64}$

Steel plate (inch)	Oxygen (lb/in²)	Propane (lb/in²)	Nozzle (special) (inch)
Up to $\frac{1}{4}$	30	3	$\frac{1}{32}$
Up to $\frac{1}{2}$	30	3	$\frac{3}{64}$

Note: for quick cutting leaving rough slag on edges, increase oxygen pressure by 5 lb per in².

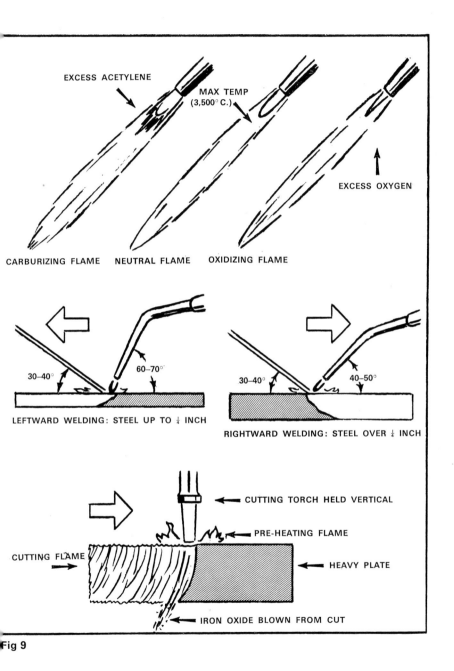

EXCESS ACETYLENE

MAX TEMP (3,500° C.)

EXCESS OXYGEN

CARBURIZING FLAME   NEUTRAL FLAME   OXIDIZING FLAME

30–40°   60–70°

LEFTWARD WELDING: STEEL UP TO ¼ INCH

30–40°   40–50°

RIGHTWARD WELDING: STEEL OVER ¼ INCH

CUTTING TORCH HELD VERTICAL

PRE-HEATING FLAME

CUTTING FLAME

HEAVY PLATE

IRON OXIDE BLOWN FROM CUT

Fig 9

Oxy-acetylene welding and oxy-acetylene or oxy-propane cutting
Note that rightward welding is more difficult. Note lag when cutting heavy iron or steel sections, shown in sectional drawing below.

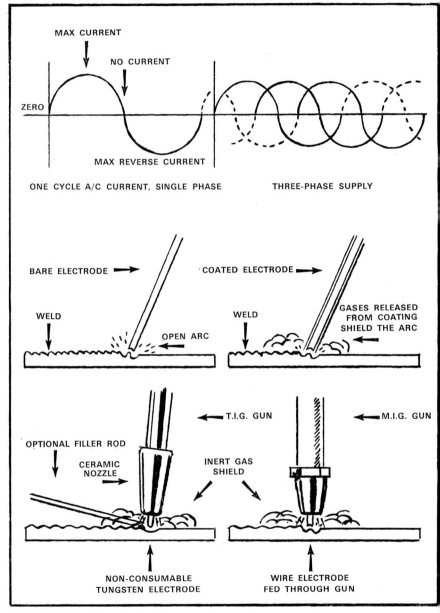

Fig 10

Electric arc welding
Above, the diagram shows why 3-phase A/C supply is more even than single-phase. Below, manual electrode welding is open to atmospheric contamination, though coated electrodes give protection by producing gases. T.I.G. and M.I.G. welding processes project a continuous stream of inert gases to form a shield around the electrode.

U.K. Buyer's Guide to Section Three (U.S. readers refer to p. 8)
Unless otherwise stated, addresses are London: branches in addition to London are in brackets.

Flame-welding and cutting equipment
        Air Products Ltd
        British Oxygen Co. Ltd (incorporating B.I.G.)
        Suffolk Ironfoundry Ltd, Suffolk
        Young & Co.

All gases
        Air Products Ltd
        British Oxygen Co. Ltd (incorporating B.I.G.)
        Distillers Co. Ltd

Electric-welding equipment; A/C, D/C, M.I.G., T.I.G. and semi-automatic
        British Oxygen Co. Ltd (incorporating B.I.G.). 'Quasi-Arc'
        Air Products Ltd
        E.S.A.B. Ltd, Kent, Birmingham (Arc specialists)
        Max-Arc Ltd, Surrey (A/C transformers only)
        Murex Welding Processes Ltd, Herts (Arc specialists)
        Messrs Gresheim Ltd (M.I.G. and T.I.G. only)
        Rockweld Ltd, Surrey

Metal-spraying equipment and services
        Metco Ltd
        F. W. Berk & Co. Ltd
        H. G. Sommerfield Ltd

Shot-blasting equipment and services
        F. W. Berk & Co. Ltd
        Guyson Industrial Equipment Ltd, Yorkshire
        H. G. Sommerfield Ltd (Leighton Buzzard)

Protective clothing: Section Eight

Grinding and polishing equipment: Section Eight

Anodizing and electroplating: Section Eight

Metals

Mild steel stockists
        Local engineering trade suppliers

Scrap steel stockists
        '600 Group' scrap yards or local scrap-metal merchants

Stainless steel stockists:
      Rankington Ltd, Essex
      Suffolk Ironfoundries Ltd, Suffolk
      London Metal Warehouses Ltd
      Taylor Stainless Metals Ltd, Buckinghamshire
      G. & F. Supplies Ltd, Middlesex

General

The development of plastics has been continuing since the end of the las century and the term plastics now covers a complex of materials of which those dealt with here form a small and relatively simple part.

Firstly, there is the vast range of thermosetting plastics materials which are manufactured as liquids in two to three component parts. These are the polyesters and epoxy resins. They require reinforcement and are formed in a one-way process.

Secondly, there is an even larger range of thermoplastics, manufactured in powder or chip form and fabricated into very thin sheets which are subsequently laminated to provide whatever thicknesses may be required. They are structural materials—either flexible or rigid—and are formed under heat in a reversible process: raise a thermoplastic object carefully to the temperature a which it was formed and it will revert through the sequence of forming operations back into a sheet.

Thermosets are built up with glass-fibre reinforcement over female mould surfaces and subsequently painted if required, though mass-pigmentation can be effected before lay-up.

Thermoplastics can be bent and formed when hot, either freely or by mechanical forming, e.g. they can be injected under pressure into moulds. These materials can be bonded with adhesives, welded together by high-frequency vibration, screwed over a frame or welded with hot gas and a filler rod. It is possible to vary the mass-pigmentation of various thermoplastics by laminating a screen-printed surface on to the rigid sheet.

Treated separately in this section, under the proper name of polymethy methacrylate, is a material which has a special translucent quality.

Part 1 · Polyester and Epoxy Resins

   I Thermosetting plastics
  II Use of additives
 III Preparation of moulds
 IV Gelcoat
  V Lamination
 VI Fillers and pigments
VII Usage

I Thermosetting plastics

Both polyester and epoxy resins are the product of organic chemistry, and have similar cured properties, but while neither could be said to look or last significantly better there are several distinguishing factors in the liquid resins. First cost: epoxy is more expensive. Then there is shelf life—poly-ester lasts about three months in prime liquid condition, epoxy indefinitely. Not so important when working into small moulds is the gel time (time taken to thicken), which in the case of polyester resin is from ten to twenty minutes on average, and for epoxy resins is about an hour.

The epoxy resin comes in two equal parts, one of which contains the curing agent (amines, polyamides, acid anhydrides), and when these portions are mixed the molecules in the resin are chopped up so as to reform as a solid. Polyester resin is referred to as 'unsaturated' in the form that concerns us, and has long chains of molecules. A small percentage of a catalyst is introduced into the viscous resin, and this causes the long molecules to join together and form three-dimensional lattice structures. Either an oven temperature, or a small quantity of a third additive are needed to make this all happen. Technically, the unsaturated polyester contains esters, styrene, stabilizers, etc., and the styrene monomer is catalysed by an organic peroxide, made reactive by the addition of cobalt napthenate.

Without the jargon, polyesters are translucent treacles which smell until cured. If the lid is left off the can, or if the resin is stored in a transparent container, the material will 'go off' very slowly—especially in sunlight, but will cure quickly with the addition of 1–4% accelerator and catalyst. Always consult a manufacturer if resin is purchased in bulk, because he will provide a range of resins for gelcoat, lamination, filling and so on, with various properties.

Polyesters are as strong as epoxy resins when air-cured, are much cheaper, more easily fabricated, and the difference in shrinkage rates is so small as to be negligible; both thermosets are dimensionally stable and have (when reinforced) structural properties which make them stronger weight for weight than steel. They are both resistant to attack by acids, etc., in the atmosphere, but epoxy resin will shed a fine white powder when exposed for years to ultra-violet light, while polyester resin will, under similar conditions, tend to make the glass reinforcement more visible: in neither case is it necessary to fill with pigments, or to cover with protective paints.

Structures can be reinforced at will by the addition of laminations and ribbing, made possible by the glass fibre associated with synthetic resins. Thermosets are super glues, while glass fibres are impervious omni-directional frameworks which give amazing flexible strength to areas. The fact that glass could be drawn into fine thread was probably known to the Egyptians, but now that marbles of glass can be drawn out cheaply into strands miles long, we have a basis for general use: these continuous filaments can be chopped up to make a random high-bulk omni-directional reinforcement used in the 'dough-mould' process. This random material can then be compressed to form a bi-directional chopped strand mat commonly used in the hand lay-up process. The filaments can also be spun into roving (rope)—used for ribbing—and the rovings can be woven to provide fabric for industrial use, where uniformity and great strength is necessary.

A small one-off racing car is likely to be fabricated with a polyester resin, reinforced with chopped strand mat by the hand lay-up process. A yacht manufactured without regard for absolute economy and to meet stringent requirements will be fabricated out of resins, reinforced with woven roving or by a spray process, and then oven-cured.

II Use of additives

Epoxy resins
The high cost and limited advantages of epoxy resins suggest that their sculptural use will be very specialized, requiring consultation with a manufacturer as to the resin and additives to be used, and the percentage quantities.

Polyester resins
Plastic bowls are moulded in polythene and polypropylene, to which (mercifully) polyesters do not stick. Resins are normally used in 1–1½-lb quantities at a time, and a 2-lb bowl will therefore allow vigorous stirring without spilling. As cure is exothermic, the room temperature will affect gel time, and this can also be altered by changing the percentage of additives (this is not the case with epoxy resins). A nomograph is provided to facilitate the translation of percentages into grams or ccs, so that it may be simply said that 1% will give a gel time of several hours in an outdoor studio in winter, while 4% will give a gel time of five or six minutes in summer sunlight. This is rather misleading, since the longer gel time will not increase the working life of the resin a great deal—it will get blobs and strings of gel after twenty minutes or so, but the time taken to cure will be greatly affected. Bulk resin can build up heat more quickly than thin layers, so this also affects gel time, while thin skins of resin lose solvents by evaporation and appear to 'go off'.

Additives for use with polyester resins have a clear function. First there is the expensive catalyst (e.g. methyl ethyl ketone peroxide), which causes the rapid formation of long chains of molecules and thus cure, or hardening. It is sometimes called hardener, sometimes catalyst, sometimes M.E.K.P. Second, we have (fortunately) another much cheaper chemical which disperses the catalyst into the resin and makes it possible to cure resin without having to put the casting into an oven: this is called an accelerator (e.g cobalt napthenate). Read the paragraph on safety and storage unless you are really familiar with peroxides.

It is the catalyst which does the work, the accelerator acts only on the catalyst. So the accelerator can safely be introduced and mixed into the resin either by the manufacturer (pre-accelerated resin) or the user, at 3–4% for gel times of about twenty minutes, more or less according to the weather, in all cases the catalyst being introduced at the same percentage only when you are ready to start work. Like most sculptors I rely on experience in the estimation of percentages, but to find out what 3% accelerator or catalyst to 1½ lb resin looks like, use a dispenser (see Buyer's Guide, p. 78) calibrated in ccs and measure off 20 ccs of each. Wash out the vessel before measuring the second additive.

Thixotropic resins and resin pastes require similar percentages of additives, but offer more resistance to their introduction. Mix accelerator into a thixotropic paste before using the paste to thicken up a body of resin. Where fillers of any kind are used, increase the percentage of additives slightly to prevent the inhibition of cure. This often applies to pigments.

Mix each additive into the resin with a thin stick before introducing the other; the stick will become loaded with resin after being used a few times.

Safety and storage

Catalysts are colourless and odourless. These organic peroxides must be kept in a sealed plastic container, labelled 'Inflammable. Poison.' Wash from skin, eyes or clothes with plenty of water. Note that M.E.K.P. is immiscible with water, and does not evaporate when spilt. If ignited, M.E.K.P. will generate oxygen and explode. May ignite spontaneously in rags. Accelerators are maroon and odourless. Disperse accelerator in 96% resin before introducing catalyst. Without a buffer, accelerator + catalyst = violent chemical reaction resulting in fire.

Resins

Epoxy resins are supplied as equal quantities of resin and catalyst resin, having unlimited storage life in sealed opaque containers. Polyester resins are supplied either pre-accelerated (maroon), or as translucent liquid. If left unsealed, or exposed to light, or stored for more than six months before use, the monomer will evaporate and leave the resin milky white. At flash point marked on the container, resin emits heavy inflammable vapours. This means that in a fire the resin becomes a time bomb. Fumes are non-toxic, but dust from sanded resin is powdered glass—see Section Seven Part 4 for notes on masks and protective clothing. To avoid discomfort during lamination, use mask with filter for organic vapours, rubber or polythene gloves, and barrier cream. Solvent is acetone.

1 Preparation of moulds (polyesters only)

The mould may be any surface which is not porous, and which is not subject to attack by the solvents present in the resin—mainly the styrene monomer. Since thermosets can glue clean glass, the separation of mould from cast is evidently a special problem.

Non-porous moulds

Apply two coats of non-silicone wax and one of release agent to all steel, aluminium, glass or polyester resin mould surfaces. Your supplier will provide the appropriate release agent according to the material, it will be a fast-drying liquid which must be smeared or sprayed evenly over the whole surface.

Porous moulds

Wooden moulds are best given two coats of polyurethane varnish (gloss), two coats of non-silicone wax and one of standard mould release agent, a wax or chemical in a solution of P.V.A. It is a fast-drying liquid which must be smeared or sprayed over the whole surface.

Plaster moulds must be dust dry before any attempt is made to seal the surface. Use shellac in two or three (or more) thin even coats until a shine is present, apply two coats of non-silicone wax (silicones react with resins), bringing each coat to a high gloss. Finish with one coat of standard P.V.A. release agent as above.

The evenness of these barriers will determine the surface texture of the cast, which is vital where mass-pigmentation is used to colour the work; polyesters can register fine differences in texture.

IV Gelcoat

The rest of this part will deal with hand lay-up of plaster moulds. Other moulds are simpler to handle though the process is essentially the same for all.

When a laminating resin is applied to the mould as a thin treacle, it will tend to run down to the lowest point before gelation, leaving a very thin coat with puddles. For this reason a gelcoat resin is manufactured with a higher viscosity (thixotropic) to ensure an even and reasonably thick coat of resin on the surface. Where this separate resin cannot be afforded, purchase a quantity of thixotropic paste, mix some accelerator into it and then mix this into ordinary non-thixotropic laminating resin to raise its viscosity. Mix (see Use of Additives Part 1 : II) the gelcoat and brush rapidly over the mould surface—it may be said that, with experience, the amount of additives in the gelcoat should be raised to allow quick gel and cut down the time between this first and all subsequent coats. Cover all of the mould surface in one mix. If the resin suddenly goes into blobs or strings stop ; leave the mould until the half-finished gelcoat has cured enough to allow it to be stripped out in one flexible sheet, reapply release agent and start again.

If the plaster mould was not bone dry when this gelcoat was applied, the lowered temperature and general ambience of the mould will cause rucks and blisters to deform the resin after gelation. Strip out the gelcoat, dry the mould with heat and start again.

Wash brushes in acetone, then soap and water or detergent. Acetone is not vital. Pour off excess resin from the mixing bowl: exothermic cure will raise the temperature of bulk resin above the tolerance of polythene of polypropylene. There are commercial preparations made for clearing off resins.

V Lamination

Within an hour of gelcoat application it should (given an ambient temperature of 65° F. and 4% additives) be dry. Touch the gelcoat—if it is coming off on the fingers still, wait. If not, lamination can proceed uninterrupted until completion.

While the gelcoat is drying, cut up a quantity of chopped strand mat. Note the tendency of glass fibre to assume an easy curve over prominent areas of the mould ; either cut the mat so as to butt up to corners, peaks, etc., or unravel the fibres where they must turn sharply. When working quickly over a wet gelcoat use a layer of glass fibre surfacing tissue before going on to matting.

Rubber gloves are necessary from now on. Coat the mould gently (so as not to pick up the gelcoat) with laminating resin (about 1½ lb per mix) and lay the glass fibre into this resin. The object now is to remove all air from the glass and replace it with resin, and as glass does not get wet this requires effort: either stipple more resin into the glass fibre and keep on until it is obviously well wetted and hard against the mould or, if the mould is fairly flat, use a washer-roller manufactured for lamination purposes. Work an area at a time, do not get too much glass into the mould or you may not have time to push all the air out of it. Any pockets of air left in the glass fibre will be voids beneath the gelcoat, which will cave in, leaving bubbles to be filled. Over a marked texture it may be advisable to build up the gelcoat with thixotropic paste to make lamination easier. Laminate one layer of glass fibre over all the mould surfaces at a time, as it is difficult to see the difference between one, two and three layers of glass fibre when building up at random.

It is virtually impossible to work to the seams with chopped strand mat, therefore overlap (Section One Part 2) the seams. These are called 'lapped edges', and ensure a full casting thickness at the seam edge, which can later be sawn and filed off.

Three laminations of chopped strand mat ($1\frac{1}{2}$ oz per ft^2) are standard for a casting up to the size of, say, an armchair; less glass fibre will increase the flexibility of the casting and its tendency to distortion, while six laminations will be sufficient to make a house.

Mould removal
Cure will be effected overnight in all but the coldest conditions. The lapped edges can be removed flush to the seams with a coping saw, a hacksaw blade or a dreadnought file. In rare instances the cast is best assembled with the mould case intact, but in the majority of cases it is best now to drop the mould a few times to break the plaster, and then to strip it away from the cast.

The optimum reinforcing ribs are made by lay-up over the cured casting surface of wire-centred paper rope or aluminium tube. If the casting is a regular form it may be necessary to screw the parts of the cast to a wood frame, using resin as a glue. In other instances it is necessary to assemble the parts and clamp edges flush to each other (distortion by warping of the plaster moulds will have made this difficult) before joining them from inside with resin and glass-fibre strips. The casting can be flexed to a certain degree to facilitate flush joints. Any struts which can be introduced will increase the strength of the casting, sharp corners can be strengthened by wrapping resin-impregnated glass fibre around a cardboard or paper tube and stippling this into the cast—the tube form gives high lateral strength. Inaccessible caps must be fitted into place with resin-impregnated strips of glass fibre left standing proud of the surface between the body and the cap section. More secure methods depend on the case in hand.

Alternative resins, treatments, finishing procedures and fillers are dealt with under 'Usage', and in Section Seven Part 1.

VI Fillers and pigments
Before making use of fillers or pigmenting resins for casting it is very necessary to be familiar with the characteristics of the brand of resin and type of additives you are using. The liquid material is quite costly, so that if you have coloured or filled a hundred pounds with the wrong proportions or with an unsatisfactory result, the waste will be considerable. Always run a test. Try mixing powdered wood, powdered metal, asbestos or plaster—indeed just about anything—with a pre-accelerated resin, and test the result in terms of (a) the effect on gel time, (b) the effect on time to cure and (c) the effectiveness of cure (by cutting and filing the surface of the casting).

Fillers most useful in giving a buttery consistency to the resin, in giving an opaque body to the appearance of the resin, or in reducing the volume cost of the resin, are those which are inert. Inert, in that they do not absorb or react with the solvents or additives in the resin, and do not move or change under a range of conditions after cure e.g.,

Powdered metals	Powdered fired clay
Silica flour	Slate powder

These examples of basically different fillers may be added in proportions up to a major fraction of the bulk of the resin, according to requirements, but will necessitate (after tests) difficult bulk dispersion to avoid unevenness, and increased additives.

Always disperse filler into a small quantity of resin, the result into a larger body of resin, and so on until the two quantities are dispersed. Leave until bubbles have risen and disappeared.

Pigments
As noted in Section Nine, the technology of surface coatings, which must embrace the mass-dispersion of pigments in polyester resins, is a vast subject. Organic and inorganic chemistry governed the limitations of European painters as they moved by a process of trial-and-error from the use of powder pigments, to water-dispersed pigments and on through water, egg-emulsion and oil (tempera) painting to oil painting. We know more now, but it is more knowledge about more media, and the user is still chasing the chemists for exact rules. Such chemists may throw up their hands, but it may now be said that some really advanced dyestuffs may be used to give translucent colour to castings without earlier fears of their being bleached out by ultra-violet light.

This means dispersing such dyestuffs which are very expensive in small quantities through a mass of polyester or epoxy resin. The alternative is to use pigments—which actually reflect light on a particular wavelength to the exclusion of all others—and are therefore not translucent but opaque, and which do not have the richness of dyestuffs since all but the light on their own wavelength is absorbed. At all events, pigments are generally more stable than dyes, do not show the chopped strand matting through the gel coat (which could be masked with surfacing tissue when using dyes), and blot out ultra-violet rays which otherwise may leach out plasticizers and stabilizers in the resin.

Manufacturers supply a range of pigments, pre-dispersed in a small quantity of stabilized resin, as a sort of paste. These are very costly per pound, but used at 0·5–8% will go a long way. Mixing is vital—use a paint-stirrer in a power drill at low speed.

VII Usage
Various sculptors have been using low reactivity fast cure resins for ten years. But just as, when one of the authors was moulding for a firm (now extinct) which was to pioneer plastic shoes, a lack of regard for the consequences of using this material (P.V.C.) led to the insistent demand that a welt, complete with stitching, be cut into the moulds for these one-piece shoes—so plastic sculpture appeared in disguise. As noted earlier, it is im-

possible to give a resilient 10-lb F.R.P. casting the quality of a 100-lb bronze casting : it is possible however to clothe the plastic in the borrowed rhetoric of more traditional media, as long as the result is seen by the sculptor as *ersatz*. This is not a question of respect, more one of adopting a plausible stance. For some people Verdi's *Aida* may seem plausible on television, with commercials, for others not. However this may be, television as a medium does not suffer but remains, as do plastics, to be exploited.

Thermosetting plastics are man-designed, and can be developed to meet almost any requirements. They are synthetic hybrids, very adaptive, relatively anonymous and nowhere near as predictable in their uses as metal or stone. The cheapness (relative to the cost of a first-class metal casting) of the process, and the fact that it can be accomplished by the sculptor, means that the conceptual and material processes can be integrated—as with welding in steel. Forms can be modelled, constructed or worked directly.

The finished work can be expected to have an indefinite life, though this is not to say that any pigments used will fare much better than those painted on to the carvings of Phidias, they may perhaps last fifty years longer.

Transparent polyesters are available, low reactivity resins for sheet fabrication (not recommended, since the glass fibres remain visible), and isothalic resins for making small solid castings without overheating due to exothermic cure.

Part 2 · Polyvinyl Chloride and Other Thermoplastics

General

Whereas those thermosetting plastics mentioned in Part 1 are purchased in liquid form, for use with additives in making any shape desired, thermoplastics are purchased ready-fabricated into sheets, including colour, in a range of thicknesses and surface textures, and can then be formed by one of the following processes. Polymethyl methacrylate (*Perspex, Oroglas, Plexiglas,* etc.) is dealt with in Part 3, as having a range of properties quite distinct from those of most other plastics materials.

The most common plastic before the chemists got to work was rubber, then came celluloid and a torrent of other more versatile materials, the most common of which is polyvinyl chloride (P.V.C.). P.V.C. is rather more expensive than steel or fabricated F.R.P. sheet for a given size of sheet, but has the advantage of needing no surface treatment (as does steel), and also of being plastic under heat (unlike F.R.P.). It is rolled out into sheets twenty thousandths of an inch thick, cut to size, and then numbers of sheets are laminated together under heat and pressure with or without polished surface(s) into sheets up to 2 inches thick. P.V.C. cannot be powdered and re-used, but a sheet can be reheated and re-formed several times before becoming brittle and discoloured. **See Section Seven Part 1 for details of properties and cost.** Polythene and polypropylene sheet are somewhat more expensive than P.V.C. in area/unit cost, but are easier to work, and are re-useable. These materials are extruded rather than laminated, are available

E

in rigid sheets up to about 6 ft × 4 ft × $\frac{1}{2}$ inch in a range of rather more translucent colours than P.V.C. P.V.C. has a service temperature of up to 60° C., and polythene has, with polypropylene, the advantage here too of being stable up to 90° C. Nylon does not come in very useful forms, and is very costly; cellulose acetate, and even cellulose nitrate are a fire risk. Another material subject to much development right now is polystyrene, usually thought of as an expanded material, but available also as a semi-rigid sheet up to $\frac{1}{4}$ inch thick. Polystyrene sheet (toughened) is very expensive as yet, and not very strong, though it has the advantage of being an excellent vacuum-moulding material, and has a range of textures distinct from the polished/unpolished P.V.C. range. All of these materials have manufacturer's trade names, lists of which appear in trade literature.

Usage

The means of usage described briefly below are:

  I Direct heat forming
  II Male force moulding
  III Vacuum forming
  IV Hot gas-welding

I Direct heat forming

It is necessary here to make an arbitrary distinction between forms which are complex and partly chance, and forms which are simple and architectonic. In general it may be said that the main difficulties experienced in modelling in thermoplastics material are discoloration and incompatibility. Architectonic forms require careful bending and joining techniques, designed to maintain structural rigidity. Discoloration will inevitably occur where complex forms are built up by the addition of small multicoloured pieces of plastic, as repeated heating will affect pigments, and may leach out plasticizers. Any form of heating is in order: soldering iron, hair dryer, oven, asbestos sheet over a gas ring, vacuum cleaner driven hot-air blower, infra-red fires or lamps and so on. **Overheating can be seen to occur when using a polished material, which will lose its gloss.** Incompatibility between, say, polythene and P.V.C. exists at the level of welding, and also in their relative softening points; polythene is also resistant to more chemicals—thus cannot be glued with an adhesive designed for P.V.C.

See Section Seven Part 1 for details of general construction.

Bending

There is a choice when bending between the heating of the whole sheet of plastic, which allows the material to form its own corner radius when bent (thus giving maximum strength), and strip heating, which facilitates economy and accuracy. Whole sheet heating is a matter of using sufficient heat over the sheet to be bent to allow it to be manhandled, or folded on a hinged working surface. The temperature, if there is any means of measurement available, should be 125–130° C. Whole sheet bending is clearly essential where a cylinder, cone or large radius bend is needed.

Crude strip heating consists simply in blanking off a part of the sheet before heaters are brought over the sheet. It is also possible to control the heating of a strip by running a hot-air blower backwards and forwards over the material (using a trolley or skid to control the height). To do the job properly, industry applies electrical heaters, with a loading of about 300 watts per foot to two mild steel bars, and these are then brought into contact with the plastic along the line of the bend, one on each side. This method is very quick, giving heating to a $\frac{1}{4}$-inch thickness in less than a minute. It is usual to let one bar into the work surface (over the hinge point) and to pivot a frame holding the upper bar so that it rests over the other on any thickness sheet of plastic, by its own weight. Illustrated are some recommended bending layouts for common architectonic shapes (fig. 14). If sheet is clamped too near corners when bending these shapes, a sharp internal bend will be achieved while the outer bend will be overstretched and weakened.

II Male force moulding

If a sheet of plastic is heated generally to around 130° C. it is possible to take advantage of the elastic properties of hot plastics, which will draw tight against any force that acts on them and stretch as evenly as possible. The simplest kind of thermoforming requires:

A A clamp, in the form of G-clamped strips or a hinged frame, to hold down the sheet, and to prevent the outsides of the sheet from being taken into the draw when forming.

B A male-forming tool, which can be anything from a stick to a relatively complex mould (no undercuts); there is no need for a female mould.

This is clearly a crude method of forming, but one which allows a range of simple shapes to be pressed into the sheet with, for instance, a wooden pattern. It may be necessary to heat both the sheet and (to a lesser extent) the surface of the forming tool. In theory, it is possible to stretch the sheet by 500%, though this depth of forming will only be achieved with a curved tool, as there is a natural tendency for the plastic to overstretch at corners. **Do not attempt to remove the pressure from the forming tool until you are confident that the temperature of the sheet has dropped near to room temperature.**

III Vacuum forming

The principle of vacuum forming is that the thermoplastic sheet is put on top of an open box, so as to form an airtight lid, heat is applied to the sheet, and air is then exhausted from the box. If the box is empty, the sheet will sink into it until it has formed a tight fit to the inside of the box, and when cooled it will maintain this shape. If any shape is placed inside the box prior to forming, the sheet will draw over this shape until air is exhausted or trapped. This basic procedure is illustrated diagrammatically (fig. 13).

Due to the absolute limitation imposed by the available force (less than one atmosphere), and the further limitation imposed by the low thermal conductivity of plastics, this process is limited to the accurate forming of sheets of $\frac{1}{16}$ inch thickness or less. For simplicity of use and ease of construction, the following general elements are necessary to a vacuum-forming table:

A Heater: in constructing a vacuum-forming table enough trouble must be taken to warrant some expenditure on heater elements. These are best obtained as infra-red ceramic trough heaters, which are about 3 inches × 9 inches; these are mounted on a frame (*Dexion* metal for example) with 1-inch clearance between each heater, giving about twelve heaters to cover 2 square feet, and a sheet of asbestos fibreboard can be mounted above the heaters to minimise heat loss upwards. This frame can then be mounted so as to slide or swivel over the vacuum-forming table as required. Such heaters have a rating of about 1·5 kW per ft^2 mounted 5 inches above the sheet. The height and the length of time for which a particular kind and thickness of plastic sheet is exposed to the heater may be advised by the manufacturer, or judged by trial and error. If a less sophisticated form of heating is used, an attempt must be made to ensure even spread of heating over the sheet.

B Drape box: this is the term for the box containing the form. In its simplest form this would be an airtight wooden box, say 2 ft × 2 ft × 8 inches deep, with a simple gasket at the top surface of the side walls. The box would contain a perforated tray, beneath which an exhaust outlet leading to the extractor would be drilled. In attempting a larger unit, it is worth considering the extra complication of allowing the perforated tray to be raised and lowered; 'drape forming' is briefly described below. Over the gasket a hinged metal frame is mounted, which will clamp the thermoplastics sheet to the gasket as an airtight fit.

C Exhaust: exhaust fans are available in a variety of shapes and sizes, perhaps the cheapest, and effective for a small table, is a cylindrical-type vacuum cleaner, which can usefully be turned round for blowing.

D Former: if the former is female, the plastic will be drawn down into shape so as to duplicate it on the visible side. This method is the simplest, and stretches the plastic less than a male former. When a male former is used, the sheet has to be pulled down at the sides over the mould, thus stretching the sheet and wasting quite an area of plastic, which has to be trimmed off. This can be reduced by the drape-forming method described below. The male or female former can be made of any material, but is best left with a fine matt finish. A gloss finish encourages the trapping of bubbles on the surface of the plastic sheet. **Wherever the former is contoured it is necessary to drill some very fine holes through it and the tray beneath.**

With some ingenuity it is possible to achieve a reproduction of very detailed shapes, though troughs will trap air unless vented, and sharp corners may catch and chill the moving plastic, cutting through them. Where it is necessary to attempt a deep form in relatively thick material, drape-forming techniques are needed and it may be possible to incorporate the following procedures: use a reversible fan or a separate blower, so that the heated sheet can be blown up into a bubble, and then raise a male former into the bubble until it touches and an airtight seal is effected in the drape box, thereafter exhaust the air in the drape box. By this means a pre-stretched sheet can be male moulded without wastage in pulling the plastic all the way down to the perforated tray around it, and a deep form can be given a more even thickness. The problem is to achieve this procedure before heat is lost in the sheet. Keep free from draughts in a generally warm atmosphere.

IV Hot gas-welding

Thermoplastics can be welded very easily, with no more than a jet of hot air and a rod of plastic of the same type as the sheets to be joined. If the weld is to be structurally sound, it is worth taking some trouble to choose a suitable point at which to make a weld, and to follow a basic procedure in preparing the materials. If this is unimportant, the plastic can virtually be modelled with the torch.

The main considerations in hot-gas welding are covered in the illustrations at the end of this section (fig. 14)—the layout of welds and the method of heating and feeding the rod.

If you have a low-pressure spray gun (Section Nine Part 2), this can be uncoupled from its turbine compressor and will provide an ideal source of air for the bending and welding torches. If you have a sophisticated high-pressure compressor outfit, this will serve the welding torch, but by reason of the low volume of air available will not feed a bending torch.

Torches

The bending torch is a very simple device which simply blows air in volume (500–1,000 litres per minute) across a heating element. The pressure is low (6 lb per in^2 or less) and the temperature adjustable from 0°–400° C. either continuously or in steps. The purpose is basic—to raise the temperature of a general area of thermoplastic sufficiently to allow bending or shaping. The torch is either a heater element plus switches fed from a radial blower (remote feed), or an integral unit of smaller capacity (which limits the area which may be heated for bending) comprising blower, heater and switches. The hot-air tool fits a number of large bore nozzles, either round or flat, the switches being used to regulate the heat as it is built up across an area of plastic.

The welding torch: this torch blow less air than the bending torch across an element, which raises the temperature to a high of 600° C. The volume of air (50–200 litres per minute) is within the range of the high-pressure compressor described in Section Nine Part 2, the pressure being regulated down to 6 lb per in^2 or lower. Cheap flame torches burning propane gas are also available—lacking somewhat in flexibility of temperature control. The purpose is to bring a local heat to bevelled edges of thermoplastic and to the welding rod so as to melt and fuse them together. The remote torch is easier to handle, comprising only heater element and switches. An integral hot-gas welding gun incorporates a blower. Various nozzles are available, and a feeder for plastic welding rod may be attached without much trouble.

Prices quoted should include accessories. These will be jets, thermostatic cut-outs, electrical cable and air hose where necessary.

Method

Plug in welding gun and switch on blower and heater elements while setting up the plastic. Determine what sort of plastic you have, and make sure that you have welding rod of the same type, and preferably, of course, of exactly the same melting point and colour. Chamfer the edges of the plastic as illustrated at the end of this section (fig. 14) with a dreadnought file or commercial chamfering tool. Degrease the surfaces with degreasing fluid.

Fit a tacking jet on to the welding gun, switch from maximum (which was used to heat up the gun) to 400 watts (about 400° C.) and adjust the airflow down to some 80 litres per min. The latter adjustment can usually be made at the rear of the gun, measurable on a sort of hydrometer (except that the float rides on a column of air) which is supplied by hot-air tool companies. This set-up enables the gun to be held like a dagger so that the fillet of hot air exiting the gun fits directly into the groove, **allowing a direct tack weld without welding rod.** Subsequently the sheet may be bent or straightened before welding commences. While tacking with sufficient pressure to groove the sheets slightly the jet may become clogged, and should be freed with a knife without opening the slit.

Exchange tacking jet for welding nozzle or speed-welding nozzle. The latter simply has a sleeve added, through which the rod feeds itself. Always allow the gun to heat up for at least three minutes before beginning to weld. With welding nozzle, hold rod and welding torch as illustrated (fig. 14), making a pendulum motion with the torch, in line with groove. Speed-welding nozzle allows one-handed welding with nozzle pressed down against plastic and may require pressure on welding rod in sleeve to prevent dragging. Weld at 400 watts position as a general guide, using 50 litres per minute or rather less. Rigid vinyl is welded at 300° C. and does not in fact melt during the process described, but softens considerably—welding temperatures for polythene and polypropylene are higher, though in practice all temperatures are determined by experience in utilizing the switch array or gas control on the gun so as to achieve a 75–85% strong joint. Some browning of the edges of the weld is acceptable. Propane gas torches are available as indicated—ensure that any flame torch keeps the coil heater flame remote from work surface or heating control may be critical during work.

Part 3 · Polymethyl Methacrylate and Foam Plastics

Polymethyl methacrylate

Simply known as Perspex in the U.K., a translucent cast thermoplastic which has been used increasingly by painters in the U.S.A. and more recently in England by Anthony Benjamin, who exploited the possibilities of Perspex as a colour/skin/structural material in a series of large sculptures. For the painters, Perspex (Oroglas, Plexiglas, etc.) is a simple material to use in that they can simply vacuum form* and then frame a sheet. Perspex is very good as a material for thermoforming—having a relatively high softening temperature, retaining all its colour and gloss through many operations. But as a structural

* Special grades of acrylic copolymer sheet are manufactured for vacuum forming.

material it suffers from the combination of a high volume cost and a molecular composition which makes it even more susceptible to 'notching' than P.V.C. While heated, the material can literally be twisted and ballooned at will, but when cool it is prone to fracture. All of the usual thermoforming methods can be employed, with the exception of welding.

Softening temperature: 110°–160° C.
Max. sheet sizes: 10 ft × 6 ft × up to $\frac{1}{2}$ inch
Max. thickness: 1 inch

Impossible in theory, in practice polymethyl methacrylate can be jointed with polyester resin and glass fibre. If using screw fixings, buffer screws with large washers. Observe notes on cutting and drilling thermoplastics. Methacrylic glues are obtainable.

Foam plastics

The common experience of foam plastics is in seat cushions, where a synthetic rubber is normally used. Much finer expanded silicone rubbers than the standard 'Dunlopillo' are available in a range of colours. But more important perhaps is the range of plastics foams, flexible and rigid. These divide into two categories: the sheet or cube form foam or expanded material, and the two-pack liquid which produces rigid foam within any cavity (such as a plaster mould).

Resin-foaming systems

Polyurethane resin-foaming systems produce a rigid foam very smartly, where a reaction of isocyanate with water liberates CO_2 which makes all the little holes. All of the requirements for the storage of polyester resin apply to this material while in liquid form. Use a dry, sealed surface mould, mix the components with a power-driven paddle (Section Seven Part 3) for 30 seconds exactly, and then pour the creaming liquid fast into the cavity. Leave for half an hour. This foam may later be used for metal casting as if it were X.P. Other types of foam use 'blowing' gasses with different properties—such as freon. It is possible to buy flexible foaming systems.

Expanded plastics

Perhaps the most common of these is expanded polystyrene. Styrene is the base material, which is made partly polymerized into little balls. Partially expanded by dry steam, then placed into a mould which is injected with more dry steam, they expand further, and when they touch sides the steam is turned off. The result is a lightweight thermoplastic material moulded to fit. It can be cut with a hot wire as illustrated (fig. 5), modelled with a hot knife, or evaporated.

This last characteristic makes X.P. the basis of the Full-Mould process developed in this country by Geoffrey Clarke, who used the method described in Section Two to produce many large architectural sculptures which would have been impractical in bronze by the *Cire Perdu* process.

Experiments are being made at present to determine the range of applications of expanded polyurethane foam (very expensive, resists the styrene monomer in synthetic resins, which makes it possible to use as a former for direct synthetic resin lay-up, as in some of the works of Phillip King), of polyethylene foam, expanded ethylene vinyl acetate (E.V.A.) and expanded neoprene and other rubbers.

Most of these expanded plastics may be bonded by means of 'Evostick', one of the adhesives supplied for fixing ceiling tiles, or with 'Bostik D' adhesive.

Softening points of thermoplastics in degrees centigrade

Material	Temperature	Specific gravity
Acrylonitrile butadiene styrene copolymer	96°	1·05
Polymethyl methacrylate	110°–160°	1·19
Polypropylene	142°	0·91
Polystyrene	89°–101°	1·06
Toughened polystyrene	73°–95°	
Polyethylene (polythene)	95°	0·94
High-density polythene	121°	0·95
Rigid polyvinyl chloride (P.V.C.)	76°	1·41–1·55
Flexible P.V.C.	—	1·25–1·5

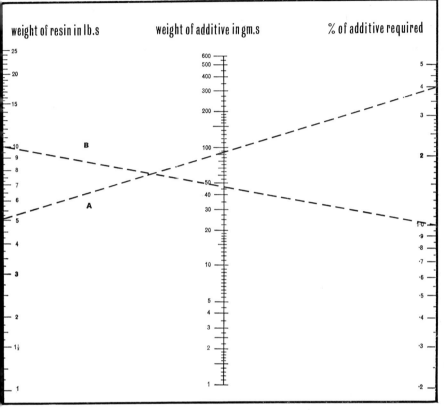

weight of resin in lb.s   weight of additive in gm.s   % of additive required

Fig 11   *(Reproduced by kind permission of B.I.P. Chemicals Ltd Birmingham)*

Nonograph For determining the amounts of catalyst and accelerator required to give a quick gel time and complete cure when using polyester resins (Part 1)

Procedure
1% additives for summer up to 4% winter. Rule a line from % **additives** scale across to **resin weight** scale and it will intersect the central scale, giving a figure. This figure may be read as the weight of accelerator or catalyst in grams, or their volumes in ccs (ml). Example A shows that 4% additives for 5 lbs resin means 88 ml (or grams) catalyst and accelerator respectively, while example B gives a weight or volume of 45.

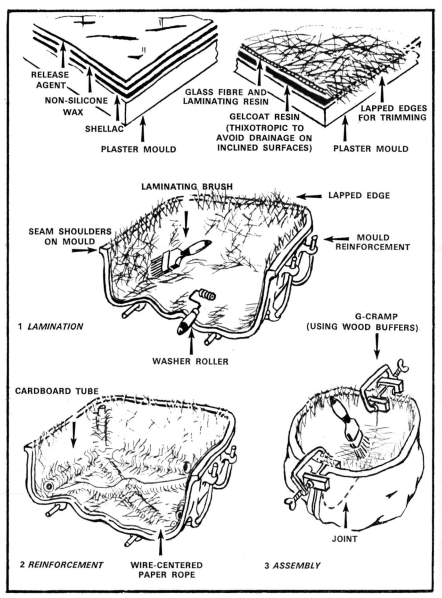

RELEASE AGENT

NON-SILICONE WAX

SHELLAC

PLASTER MOULD

GLASS FIBRE AND LAMINATING RESIN

GELCOAT RESIN (THIXOTROPIC TO AVOID DRAINAGE ON INCLINED SURFACES)

LAPPED EDGES FOR TRIMMING

PLASTER MOULD

LAMINATING BRUSH

LAPPED EDGE

SEAM SHOULDERS ON MOULD

MOULD REINFORCEMENT

1 *LAMINATION*

G-CRAMP (USING WOOD BUFFERS)

WASHER ROLLER

CARDBOARD TUBE

JOINT

2 *REINFORCEMENT*

WIRE-CENTERED PAPER ROPE

3 *ASSEMBLY*

Fig 12

Casting in polyester resin (with or without pigments) from a plaster mould
Dry and prepare the mould thoroughly. Paint a gelcoat into the mould over parting agent. When hard, paint in laminating resin and glass fibre: impregnate fibres by stippling and rolling. Reinforce when hard with paper rope or tube, overlaid with resin/glass fibre. Assemble in mould where possible, after trimming off lapped edges.

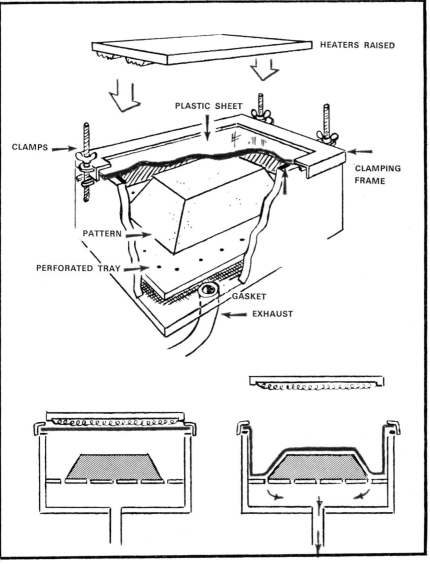

HEATERS RAISED

PLASTIC SHEET

CLAMPS

CLAMPING
FRAME

PATTERN

PERFORATED TRAY

GASKET

EXHAUST

Fig 13

Simple vacuum forming of P.V.C. sheet, etc.

A wood or plaster pattern sits on a perforated tray. Plastic sheet is clamped to the vacuum bed over an air-tight gasket, heat is applied and the air exhausted. Infra-red bathroom heater or gold-plated ceramic elements, vacuum pump or vacuum cleaner—the principles remain simple.

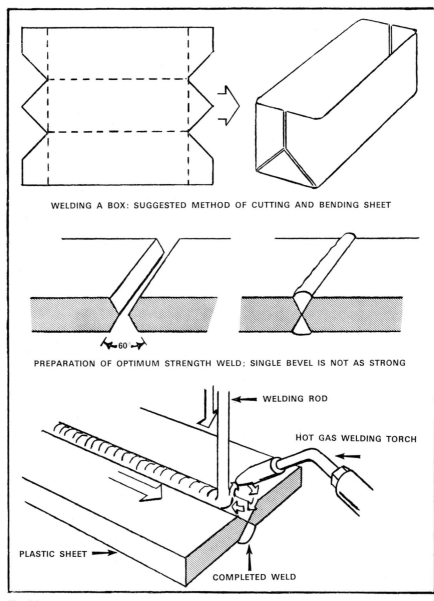

WELDING A BOX: SUGGESTED METHOD OF CUTTING AND BENDING SHEET

PREPARATION OF OPTIMUM STRENGTH WELD; SINGLE BEVEL IS NOT AS STRONG

WELDING ROD

HOT GAS WELDING TORCH

PLASTIC SHEET

COMPLETED WELD

Fig 14

Hot gas welding of thermoplastics

Welding rod must be of similar material to sheet. Use torch to heat both bevelled joint and welding rod in continuous motion. Gently press rod vertically into vee. Some discolouration may occur at weld.

Buyer's Guide to Section Four (U.S. readers refer to p. 8)
Unless otherwise stated, addresses are London: branches in addition to London are in brackets.

Reinforced plastics manufacturing suppliers

Epoxy resins
        Bakelite Ltd
        British Industrial Plastics Ltd, Birmingham
        Ciba (A.R.L.) Ltd. 'Araldite'
        Shell Chemical Co. Ltd. 'Epikote'
        Croxton & Garry Ltd, Surrey. 'Omya'

Polyester resins
        Artrite Resins Ltd, Surrey
        Bakelite Ltd
        Beck, Koller & Co. Ltd, Liverpool. 'Fillabond'
        British Industrial Plastics Ltd, Birmingham. 'Beetle'
        British Resin Products Ltd
        Scott, Bader Ltd, Northamptonshire. 'Crystic'

Catalysts and accelerators
        Resin manufacturers
        Novadel Ltd
        Perox Chemicals Ltd

Dispersed pigments for polyesters
        Cellon Ltd, Surrey
        Geigy (U.K.) Ltd, Manchester
        Llewellyn Ryland Ltd, Birmingham
        Reeves & Son Ltd, Middlesex

Glass fibre
        Deeglas Fibres Ltd, Surrey
        Fibreglass Ltd, Birkenhead
        Fothergill & Harvey Ltd, Lancashire

Fillers
        English China Clays (Sales Co.) Ltd, Cornwall
        Lonabarc Ltd
        Metallic Paints and Powders Ltd
        Berk Ltd

Brands of filler paste based on resins
        'Cataloy'
        'Isopon'
        'Tetrasyl'
        'Bondapaste'
        'Devcon'

Accessories—wire-centered paper rope, dispensers, etc.
> K. & C. Mouldings Ltd, Norfolk. 'Downland'
> **Information from the Scientific Press Ltd**

Kit suppliers
> Bondaglass Ltd, Surrey
> Alec Tiranti Ltd

Resin spraying equipment
> Berk Ltd
> K. & C. Mouldings Ltd, Norfolk. 'Downland'
> Hamilton Machinery Sales Ltd. 'Polyspray'

Thermoplastics and thermoforming equipment

Acrylics
> Imperial Chemical Industries Ltd. 'Perspex', rigid sheet
> Lennig Chemicals Ltd. 'Oroglas', rigid sheet
> Cellon Ltd, Surrey. Paints and resins

Polyolefin
> B.X. Plastics Ltd, Essex. 'Bexthene' polyethylene (polythene)
> Local suppliers

Styrene
> B.X. Plastics Ltd, Essex. 'Bextrene' toughened polystyrene
> Mosanto Ltd. 'Polyflex' polystyrene

Vinyl
> Bakelite Ltd. 'Vybac' P.V.C. sheet
> B.X. Plastics Ltd, Essex. 'Velbex' rigid, 'Welbex' flexible P.V.C.
> Storeys of Lancaster
> Local suppliers

Thermo-forming tools

Vacuum forming services
> Fogg & Marten Moulds Ltd
> Omega Plastics Ltd, Essex

Vacuum forming equipment
> T. H. & J. Daniels Ltd, Gloucestershire
> John Kimbell & Co. Ltd
> **Information from the Scientific Press Ltd**

Hot gas welding equipment:
> Associated Electrical Industries Ltd
> Goodburn Plastics Ltd, Uxbridge
> Rediweld Ltd, Sussex
> Fissons Scientific Apparatus Ltd, Leicestershire
> Welwyn Tool Co. Ltd, Hertfordshire

Part 1 · Cement and *Ciment Fondu*

Part 2 · Carving in Stone

Part 3 · Carving in Wood

Part 1 · Cement and *Ciment Fondu*

General

All cements are very fine calcinated powders which harden rapidly when mixed with water, but tend to crack or craze at the surface, and generally exhibit rather a fragile character in raw form. The addition of an aggregate—rocks, brickbats, pebbles, gravel, sand, brickdust, etc.—gives the cured material a range of characteristics in relation to the coarseness of the aggregate, and the ratio of the aggregate to the cement. Portland cement sets 'green' overnight and takes a couple of weeks to cure, and rapid hardening Portland takes half this time. This cement is grey, and dense enough to make a fair registration of detail down to about $\frac{1}{16}$ inch across. Portland also supply a white cement which must be used with silver sand as aggregate to preserve its whiteness—which is slightly dearer. The French developed a very rapid hardening (8 hours) aluminous cement of extremely fine consistency and high density, *Ciment Fondu*, which costs about twice as much as standard cements, and which is recommended to sculptors as the more permanent and useful type. It is available in black or white. *Fondu* will register detail down to finger prints with care, and is about as hard as cast iron.

Direct working

This is not easy, but is the fastest and cheapest method of executing large commissioned work. A welded steel armature, coated with waterproof bituminous black paint and given bulk with a fine chicken wire mesh (use gloves and an efficient cutter, as Section Seven Part 2) provides a surface over which to build up the material thickness. Holding up the cement or *Fondu* while setting can be facilitated by shredding chopped strand matt (Section Four Part 1) into the first coat, and applying with trowel, leaving the surface as coherent as possible; any fine mesh such as scrim, expanded metal or even cloth will help to prevent the cement from penetrating the armature and falling down.

Mix the cement with three parts sharp or silver sand, or two parts sand and one part of almost any fine dust, e.g. marble, brick or stone, adding a strong powder colour by experiment if required. Then add water gradually, mixing well, until the cement is just wet enough to squeeze in the hand so as to retain the shape when released. Note that wet cement is almost impossible to work directly, and that if it is too dry it will tend to crumble. Dry mix cement and aggregates in bulk to avoid variations in tone and colour.

Cement and *Fondu* from plaster moulds

Cement casts can easily be made by the methods described for taking plaster casts from plaster moulds (Section One Parts 2 and 3), the differences being

A the strength and weight of cement, and
B preparation of mould surfaces.

A. The strength of the material allows the use of a very strong mould, without the use of any separating agent, as the mould will distintegrate under impact much faster than any cement. Because of the need to keep down the weight of the cement, it is unwise to make a solid cast—if this is done, the assembled mould can simply be poured full of runny cement, and left to harden for as long as possible. 'Rolling' is impractical, so the easiest method is to build up a 1–2-inch (very even) thickness of cement over the disassembled mould surfaces, leaving the seams clear as illustrated. Use chopped strand matt and iron bars for reinforcement at strategic points, ensuring that they will not foul opposing surfaces on assembly. It is here that you need a strong mould: it is necessary to tamp the cement into a coherent mass at the mould surface, the cement being mixed as described under Direct Working above. Use the clenched fist or a bunched damp rag.

B. The preparation of mould surfaces is not necessary as far as releasing the finished cast is concerned, but determine the nature of the cast cement surface. In setting, cement generates considerable heat, releasing water and taking in various minerals from the plaster mould. If the plaster mould is dry, this will ruin the cast by drying the cement before it has cured—if, on the other hand, it is soaking wet, the cement cast will later bloom with a white layer of minerals previously absorbed from the plaster. Nothing will stop this happening if the cast was made from a water-soaked plaster mould: this bloom is very attractive when encouraged over traditional forms, but may not be required where a relatively bland or mechanical surface is aimed at. In this case it is necessary to seal the plaster surface absolutely against both water and the effects of heat from exothermic cure. Three good coats of shellac over the mould surface when dust dry, followed by three good coats of a hard wax burnished to a gloss, followed by a thin wipe of clean oil, will prevent penetration in most cases, though a thick cast in *Fondu* may take mineral deposits even through this surface during cure. Do not wet the mould in this last case until the whole process of sealing is complete, but then a damp mould will reduce suction of water from the cement.

If the mould is not prepared, keep soaking wet during and after filling. If prepared, tamping may prove difficult, as the cement will tend to slip off the oiled surface: rubbing it into this surface with the hand will help to make it stick before you begin tamping.

When the mould parts have been filled, mix a two-parts sand to one-part cement quantity rather wetter than for the main filling process, add Unibond, and lay around the seams. It is now necessary to squeeze the mould parts together, which may call for strength: use dogs first, followed by ropes, used wet (they will shrink as they dry), which themselves can be tightened by driving wedges between the rope and mould. Try to reinforce all seams on the inside with glass fibre and iron bars, leaving the smallest caps until last.

It is common practice to undertake large sculptural commissions on a strictly commercial basis, where an architect wishes to have large areas of wall space decorated—taking advantage of the nature of cement. When a wall is rendered with a buttery mix of cement (add one part lime or plasticizer), the 'green' rendering can be cut and modelled for some hours before setting. An alternative exists in the fabrication of an interlocking set of shallow prepared plaster or reinforced plastic moulds, from which several copies may be taken in cement, using glass-fibre reinforcement and ensuring a rough but flat plane at rear of casting; this set of castings can then be mounted rather like wall tiles, using a strong mix containing a bonding agent as an adhesive.

F

Part 2 · Carving in Stone

Various sculptors during this century have continued to work in stone, and have come to terms with the slowness and monolithic emphasis that this entails, notably Fritz Wotruba, Henry Moore and Jean Arp. Constantin Brancusi reinvented the use of stone, releasing its 'stoneness' by contrast in combined entities using wood, metal and stone. The essential *methods* employed by these artists are those of previous generations, and these will be very briefly outlined below: further details for those who wish to make a deeper study of the craft are readily available in works already published.

The basic rock formations: those formed from a molten mass, the igneous rocks—such as granite; rocks formed by the accretion of generations of skeletal structures and other deposits, called sedimentary—such as sandstone and limestone (York stone is this type, used for sharpening chisels); metamorphic rocks—just that, rocks which have been subjected to such heat and pressure that they have undergone a metamorphosis into, say, marble. Soft stones are very difficult to carve, being soapy—Caen for instance or, like Bath stone, much like lump sugar. It is easier to handle a fine, coherent stone such as a Portland, which is readily available, or a marble. Granite is something to tackle with reservation, being so hard as to resist normal chisels and saws. Note that 'York', 'Bath', 'Caen', etc., are European stone quarries, not types.

When embarking on a carving which has been preconceived, it is well worth following the basic pattern suggested here: dress the stone into a block, mark off a basic silhouette on the front of this block, and drive this silhouette straight through to the back, without fussing about rounding off the shape. Then chalk the side view silhouette on to the now modified side of the block, and drive this shape through to the other side too. In this way you remove the bulk of the stone, without being lost or misled by the appearance of the stone.

There are four basic kinds of chisel:

A The pitcher, which is bent at the neck, and has a front face about $\frac{1}{8}$ inch thick. The pitcher is used first, to burst away large lumps of stone.

B The point. This chisel is used second, to drive channels across the rough stone surface to a required depth at regular intervals.

C The claw, a set of teeth allow stone to pass between them, making carving quick and accurate—used to dress the surface after it has been channelled with a point.

D The cutting chisel, which can be a straight or cupped blade, not always used, but an alternative to abrasion for finishing. There is a tendency for beginners to start and finish with a cutting chisel, a slow and impractical method.

These chisels are available for use either with a mallet or lead dummy, or in another form, with a sharp rear end, for use with a lump hammer. It is better to get used to the weight of the lump hammer, and let it do the work, than to bash away with the lighter mallet. Hammers having toothed panes are also available for bruising stone away over rounded surfaces: 'bouchard'.

Hold the chisel lightly in the whole of the left hand, with the blade at a rather sharp angle to the stone, and hit it firmly and regularly with the lump hammer: if it skids off the stone, increase the angle towards 90°; if it digs in, lower the angle. In this way the cutting is controlled almost entirely by the left hand altering the cutting angle, without having to grip the chisel very hard. Note that certain fine metamorphic stones, such as marble and gypsum (alabaster), are prone to stun. That is to say that a bruise will be carried down into the stone, and will be recorded as a white fluffy mark when the stone is polished. Examples of what can, nevertheless, be done with alabaster can be seen in the collection of English carvings in the Victoria and Albert Museum, London.

It is worth being systematic about carving, to work the whole carving down to the planes and rough size as quickly as possible. It is all too easy to go on for days recarving bits and pieces closer and closer to the finished size, which cutting could have been accomplished in two stages, using first the point and then the claw, leaving any 'finishing' until the proper time.

Small pieces of stone can be roughed up at the base, wetted, and plastered on to larger chunks, to stop them skidding about, or can be sat in a box of sand. Large pieces can be sawn with a rip saw. Alternatively, cut a distinct line around the proposed division with the pitcher and drill a row of large holes directly into the stone, using a stone drill. The stone can now be burst by driving wedges down into the holes. Stone will split at the point where a line has been cut into it in an almost uncanny way. When the stone is of the right size, you can get it up on to a banker without assistance by using a heavy lever, placing blocks alternatively under one side and then the other. The trick is to use a steel bar or wooden roller to move the stone across on to the work surface when it has been levered up to the correct height. Try removing convex areas by holding the claw or chisel at right-angles to the stone; strike at $\frac{1}{2}$ inch intervals.

Use a dust mask and a pair of cotton gloves—much more useful than a smock or beret, as you cannot brush or wash away blisters, or silica on the lungs. If you need to see the sort of furniture used to support large carvings, try looking into a local art school. It might be said that a turntable, mounted on a spider (two crossed arms bearing rollers, sandwiched between two heavy boards) is likely to be an expensive item, as demand is relatively small. See Buyer's Guide and illustration, fig. 17.

Part 3 · Carving in Wood

As with stone, it is very much easier to carve a hard, coherent wood than one which is soft or very light. Coniferous woods tend to be rather soft, though this is a generalization which does not take account of yew for instance. Deciduous woods (trees which shed their leaves in winter) are usually rather more dense, which is probably something to do with the time they take to grow. So hardwoods, as a category, are deciduous, heavy, and expensive while softwoods are generally bought as ill-seasoned pine at a modest price.

It is difficult to get hold of hardwood for carving, as the time taken to season the timber is usually such as to make it unprofitable to merchants. So you are likely to find that a log which you have bought, or have been given, will split and warp as it looses moisture. If you are very patient, a new-sawn log can be seasoned over a period of a few years in the garden, and then in the studio, but most people have to start off with a less romantic but more readily available kiln-dried baulk of timber. Any wood can be carved, provided it looks and feels fairly dry at the cut when sawn, though it is likely that a certain percentage of wood will have to be discarded because shakes appear or it splits and tears.

Various tools are needed for the woodcarver—tools for holding the wood, for cutting it, for carving it and for abrading the surface, but go easy: there is little point in taking six weeks to carve a shape which could have been modelled and cast in one. Make up your mind to use the wood on its own terms, and this means (for the most part at all events) cutting through the fibrous longitudinal grain with the largest chisel that will do the job: two or three gouges, deep gouges shaped into a U, are more valuable than a host of small shallow ones, and you will make life much easier if you get a grindstone (electric, with guard), and a set of carborundum oilstones right away. The importance of the electric grindstone lies in its speed, which allows you to concentrate on getting the chisel ground at the right angle—about 25°—evenly around its leading edge until any nicks are passed. The oilstone is best mounted for constant use in a wooden pallet, plus a can of oil, and used to keep the chisels in use really keen.

The kinds of chisel used for woodcarving, and the method of sharpening are illustrated at the end of this section (fig. 18). As the oilstone and slipstone sharpening produces a wider bevel, and as the cutting edge, seen from the side, becomes wavy, it is necessary to grind the chisel or gouge in two operations: first introduce the cutting edge to the grindstone at right angles and cut back the blade until it is straight, then grind until an even line of squared-off blade shows from the front. The tool is then ready for sharpening. Always keep the slipstone flat in the groove of the tool, so as to avoid producing a bevel on the inside edge.

As a rough and general guide, it may be said that the best woods for small, highly detailed carving are those which take a long time to grow; the bulk of these woods are those which come from trees bearing fruit or nuts. For large work it is usually necessary to utilize kiln-dried furniture-making woods, available in fairly large baulks which can be assembled into volumes. The latter woods—mahogany, oak, teak for instance—may be glued together with a casein resin glue so as to produce the basis for an extensive work. The baulks of timber must be planed and matched two or three at a time, with some attempt to keep the colour matching and grain in line. Note that there is a direction to the grain—in one plane the wood will cut along the grain more cleanly than it will if the same cut is attempted in reverse. When two pieces are to be joined, boil up some resin glue (or use the powdered casein glue sold in tins for ease) apply to both surfaces and use clamps to pressure the woods together. Cracks and holes can be filled at the same time by mixing sawdust from the wood in hand with the resin glue and using it as a paste. Leave overnight to harden before removing clamps.

Wood built up into volumes in this way will allow almost any size or configuration to be tackled; it will be found that it is difficult to detect the resin glue bonding lines after the carving has been completed.

Faults
When making small carvings, faults must simply be cut out of the wood: boxwood or cherry and other very fine, dense woods will very likely be without soft heartwood, hollow knots or shakes, but pine, cedar and even poor mahoganies may develop shakes (radial cracks wider towards the outer face). On larger work clearly faults must be corrected. Knots should be drilled and a length of dowel driven home into the hole with resin glue, before sawing-off excess. Shakes developing as a result of studio humidity may reappear after filling with sawdust and resin glue—saw out section and clamp in fresh wood.

Joints
Where a section of timber is to be joined to the bulk of a carving so as to provide the basis for a largely separate form, it will not be sufficient just to glue it on, as, for instance, the fixing of a cross-member to an upright section. Cut off square and recess into main section, clamping the pieces together firmly; drill out hole/s through both pieces of wood so that dowels may be driven through to form anchors. Disassemble and glue joints before re-assembly with clamps.

Finishing is dealt with in Section Eight Part 1.

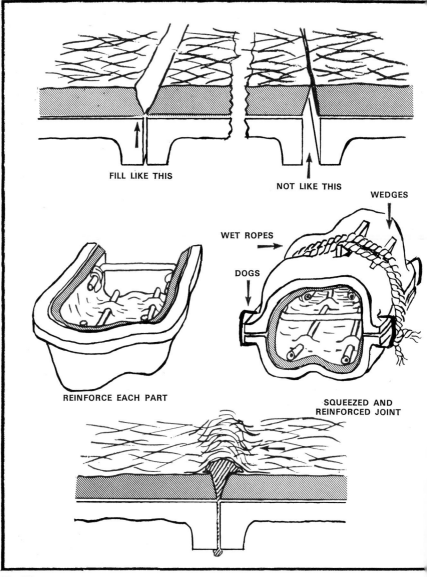

FILL LIKE THIS

NOT LIKE THIS

WEDGES

WET ROPES

DOGS

REINFORCE EACH PART

SQUEEZED AND
REINFORCED JOINT

Fig 15

Casting in cement from a plaster mould

Pre-fill the mould parts, tamp down, reinforce with scrim or glass fibre and then meta armature. Keep seams clear or parts will not fit. Run cement and Unibond adhesive aroun seams and squeeze parts together. Tie securely with wet rope, wedge, reinforce accessibl seams and leave under wet sacks for three days to a week.

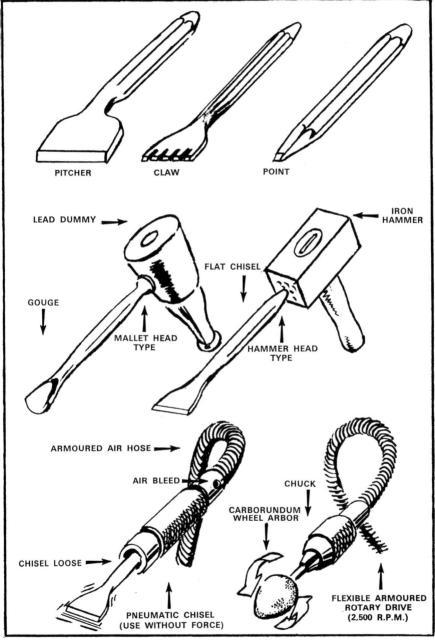

Fig 16

Various means of working stones.

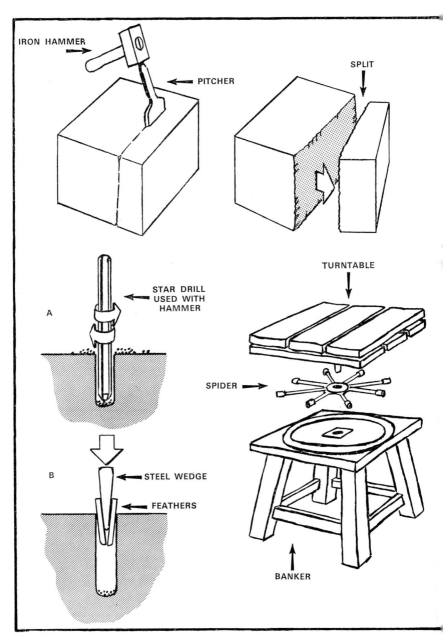

Fig 17

Splitting stone
If the block is too big to burst with the pitcher, use a star drill to make a row of holes along
the line marked by the pitcher and burst with wedges. 'Feathers' are half-round iron fillets
On the right a heavy banker.

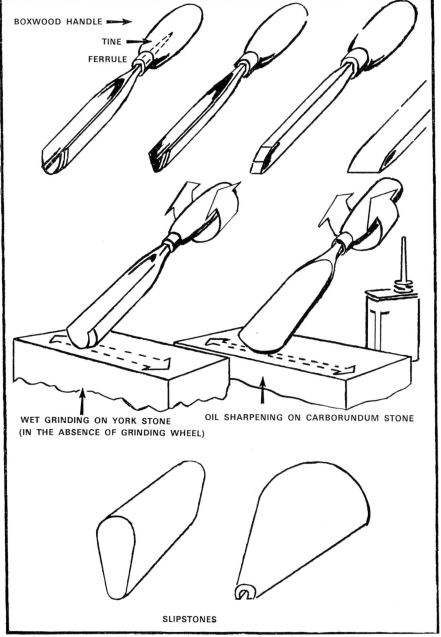

Fig 18
Woodcarving gouges and chisels: grinding and sharpening
Grind at 20° side to side. Sharpen an even strip at 25°. Clean off burr on reverse edge with one of the appropriate sizes of slipstone. Always use a gouge having a 'U' deep enough to allow fast cutting without burying itself.

Buyer's Guide to Section Five (U.S. readers refer to p. 8)
Unless otherwise stated, addresses are London: branches in addition to London are in brackets.

Heavy furniture—benches, turntables, bankers, etc.
    Alec Tiranti Ltd
    Odoni Equipment Ltd
    Parry & Sons (Tools) Ltd

General accessories
    Alec Tiranti Ltd

Stone and woodcarving chisels
    Alec Tiranti Ltd
    Skelland, Walter Ltd, Manchester

Additives and adhesives
    Unibond Ltd, Surrey. 'Unibond'
    Ciba Ltd, Cambridgeshire. 'Araldite'

Colourants for cements
    Colikeni Ltd
    Ralph Nye, Biddle & Co. Ltd
    Plycol Ltd, Buckinghamshire

Cements
    Lafarge Aluminous Cement Co. Ltd. *Ciment Fondu*
    The Cement Marketing Co. Ltd. 'Portland Blue Circle'

Stones
    The Portland Stone Co.
    Local mason's yards
    Regional stone and granite quarries

Pneumatic tools
    Compressors—Section Nine
    Pneumatic Tool Service Ltd
    Consolidated Pneumatic Tool Co. Ltd

Timber
    See under 'Hardwood Merchants & Agents' for local suppliers

Section Six · REPETITION CASTING

Part 1 · Gelatine Moulding

Part 2 · Vinyl Resin Moulds

Part 3 · Rubber Latex Moulding

Part 1 · Gelatine Moulding

General

Gelatine is the substance produced in stewing the skin, tendons, bones, etc., of various animals—a jelly which is soft when cold and liquid when hot. It is sold in brittle shards, and these must be soaked in water for 24 hours before use. They may be used repeatedly, and new gelatine can be added to old. As the material is subject to evaporation and organic decay, it must be stored in polythene, and old gelatine can be preserved by the addition of a small quantity of formalin when melted. The gelatine will, nevertheless, gradually lose its properties and be discarded.

It should be noted that various synthetics, based on rubber and on thermoplastics, are now available which are not subject to such rapid decomposition as gelatine, and which do not harden by evaporation (see Parts 2 and 3). They also have higher melting points, avoiding the problem of removing a plaster cast from the gelatine mould before it is damaged by exothermic cure.

Nevertheless, gelatine offers a very cheap means of producing up to twelve very detailed reproductions in wax or plaster, and is used widely in bronze foundries.

Moulding

As the essential quality of gelatine is its flexibility, it is clearly necessary to seat a gelatine mould in a rigid plaster jacket: its elasticity is only an advantage when removing the mould from the pattern, or from subsequent castings. It is necessary to make this jacket before making the gelatine mould, hence the following rather involuted method:

A Treat the pattern so as to make it non-porous. For example: if you wish to copy a bronze sculpture, it is already impervious, while a plaster shape would need to be brought to a shiny finish with as few and as thin coats of shellac or polyurethane varnish as possible. Now consider whether it will be possible to remove the jacket in one piece from the pattern (e.g. a relief), or in two pieces (e.g. any generally round shape), or more. **Note that undercuts are not really significant, as the mould material is flexible.** Draw the dividing line or lines on to the original, lay it down on a lump of clay so as to leave one half of the mould above the line facing up, and build up a rough wall of clay to the seam, smoothing it off at 90° to the mould surface and about $1\frac{1}{2}$ inches wide. This process can also be followed diagramatically at the end of this section (figs. 19, 20).

B Now lay a clay skin broadly over the pattern: this clay will later be exchanged for gelatine, so make sure that where the gelatine will have to be pulled to flex it out of undercuts it is thicker, and also that the surface of the clay is smooth. The best way to do this quickly is to use a rolling pin and french chalk on a wooden bench, with two strips of wood about $\frac{1}{2}$ inch thick spaced to the width of the roller—this will give you smooth, even clay sheets which can be laid over the form easily, or cut into strips where marked curves must be negotiated. If the pattern is large—say 2 feet wide and long, increase the clay thickness to 1 inch. Roll out some rats' tails of clay, and some thick slightly conical pieces, and place these as in the illustrations: they will be the holes through which the gelatine is poured, the rats' tails provide a rib at the edge of the seam all around the mould. Keep the risers and the feeder over the highest parts of the form.

C Build up a strong, neat jacket of plaster over the clay, having a cross-section as that in the diagrams. Square off the tops of feeders and push a nail or wire through the cheesy plaster as illustrated. This will later support the gelatine mould when there is no pattern inside to hold it up.

D Invert the entire thing, remove supporting clay, clay wash (Section One Part 3) the plaster jacket seam and smooth the exposed clay seam. Repeat the operation, as paragraphs B and C. Locating keys can now be cut into the jacket seams by rotating a table knife to produce a negative dimple at intervals, these will be cast off when the second part of the jacket is built up, and will enable jacket parts to fit properly together later.

E Invert again, remove the first jacket without disturbing the second (a three-piece gelatine mould is something for the expert) by prising up. Remove the clay skin and clean the pattern. You now have an exposed portion of pattern, a thin section of exposed clay skin and alongside that the seam of the other half of the jacket. Shellac this seam and then lightly oil the whole thing (rapeseed oil is recommended). Shellac and oil the inside surface of the separated jacket, replace it and dog firmly, adding string, rope, etc. until secure. Seal the seam with generous rolls of clay and make generous bungs of clay for the risers and for the feeder, and make a clay collar for the feeder. Remove pins.

F Boil water in a large container, insert a smaller container within the larger, and into the latter chop 1-inch or 2-inch cubes of gelatine, or well-soaked shards if it is new. When there is more than enough to fill the space previously occupied by the clay skin, wait until the whole evil brew is melted (no lumps at all).

G When everything is ready, remove the liquid gelatine and stand out of any draught to cool until you can insert a finger into it without discomfort. If you have asbestos fingers, note that it is too hot if it all runs off like treacle; if you are apprehensive, remember that it is too cold if it sticks to your finger in strands. Pour as evenly and as quickly as possible into the feeder until the gelatine appears in the neck of the riser/s. Cover the openings with the clay bungs. Top up as necessary, and insert pins. Leave overnight to cool.

H Now invert the whole case again, removing the second half of the jacket, and repeat E, F, G. When this half of the mould has been filled with gelatine, and has cooled, the case can be opened (remove pins first), and the inside of the jackets given a dusting of french chalk. The second pour of gelatine will have melted into the first, and they can be cut apart at the visible seam line. Dust the positive with french chalk and store with the positive contained in the mould, and the jackets on.

Part 2 · Flexible Vinyl Resin Moulds

These casting materials based on vinyl resins give excellent detail from any sort of pattern which can stand a temperature of 120°—170° C., are flexible proof against water, and do not suffer organic decomposition. The U.K. manufacturer, Vinatex Ltd, provides purpose-built thermostatic heaters to achieve controlled melting, and gives users detailed advice on method.

Do not attempt to melt Vinyl compounds in a two-pot container where the outer container is filled with oil or water—the temperature will not rise sufficiently. Use an empty outer container, and measure temperature rise of the compound if possible.

Moulds can thus be made from wood (sealed with Furane resin), plaster (sealed with shellac), metals or plastics; moulds can be filled with plaster cement, reinforced plastics.

Part 3 · Rubber Latex Moulding

Synthetic rubbers incorporating vinyl resins or latex are obtainable from the rubber companies. They are supplied with information on usage, which is basically to introduce the liquid into a mould and then heat it to achieve a once only cure. The latex-based moulding compounds contain stabilizers, preservatives (ammonia being a characteristic smell of latex moulds), gelling agents and vulcanizing agents. Vulcanizing agents allow the partly dried latex to be baked to a hard but flexible quality; this means that the latex, which is a thin milky fluid, can be introduced in the mould at leisure to ensure the removal of bubbles and filling of all detailed parts of the mould, before being allowed to dry slowly and baked. The drying may take over a week, with substantial shrinkage. Substances vary a good deal but will bake generally in a low domestic oven. These notes are intended to refer to latex used as a repetition casting mould, where it is treated as if it were gelatine or Vinamold as far as jackets are concerned: however it is likely that the rubber will shrink during cure to the point at which the jacket container is too large to be useful, and it is also likely that the latex mould will be tough enough to support itself while being filled (given that the two halves are firmly clipped together), so that after cure in the oven the jacket may be discarded. Latex used in this manner is best used approximately $\frac{1}{4}$ inch thick on small, detailed objects.

It is also possible to build up a latex thickness in separate coats over a positive by brushing or spraying. Allow each coat to dry thoroughly before applying the next. Manufacturers will advise on available fillers to body out the outer coats of latex. Applied in this fashion the latex mould can have a jacket cast over it before removal by incision and peeling—since the jacket is applied after the latex has dried, shrinkage will largely have taken place and the jacket will remain useful as a support. Up to 200 repetitions in plaster are possible from a latex mould which has properly been cured. Note that cure is achieved when a hard object pressed into the rubber leaves no impression when removed, and that any crystalline eruption at the surface of the mould after series-casting in plaster can be removed with an alcohol mixed into glycerine or castor oil.

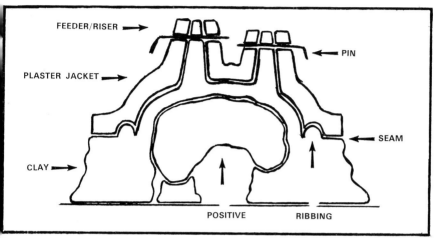

Fig 19

Gelatine moulding

The pattern of wood, metal or plaster has been dusted with french chalk and supported with clay so that a seam can be built up around the form. A clay skin is laid over the form. Then a locating rib is laid around the inside of the seam, and the feeders and risers located at the highest points. The plaster jacket can then be built up, as shown. Finally wire pins are pushed through the feeders and risers.

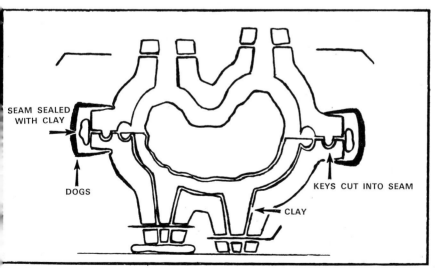

Fig 19

Here the whole thing has been inverted and the second half of the jacket built over a clay skin. One half of the jacket has been removed, the clay skin removed and the inside of the jacket and seams shellacked. The jacket and pattern are now oiled and clamped together ready for pouring the gelatine.

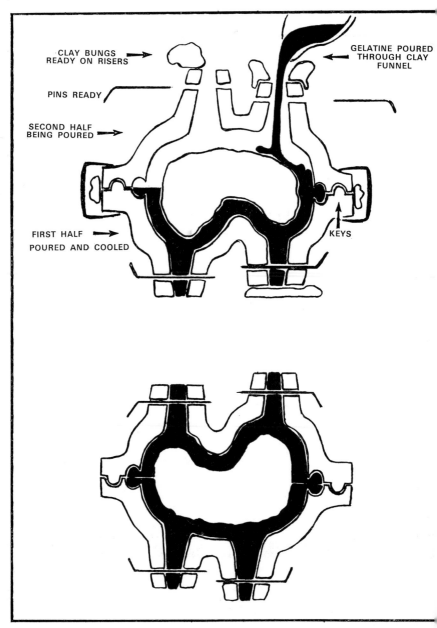

Fig 20

Pouring the second half with gelatine. Note that keys cut into the jacket seam give accurate location in these later stages. When the gelatine fills the jacket block feeders and risers with clay bungs. Top up if level falls.

The completed gelatine mould, cut in two around the seams, hangs on the pins within the jacket. Keys in jacket seams and the rib running around the gelatine seam ensures accurate location. Vinamold procedure is very similar, but the second pour does not stick to the first.

U.K. Buyer's Guide to Section Six (U.S. readers refer to p. 8)
Unless otherwise stated, addresses are London: branches in addition to
London are in brackets.

Materials other than flexible moulding compounds are to be found in the
Buyer's Guide to Sections One, Four and Five.

Flexible moulding compounds
    Vinatex Ltd, Surrey
    Dunlop Rubber Co. Ltd, Chemical Products Division

G

Part 1 · Plastics, Wood and Metal—Characteristics

Part 2 · Specialized Hand Tools

Part 3 · Power Tools

Part 4 · Personal Protective Equipment

Part 1 · Plastics, Wood and Metal—Characteristics

(N.B. The details here are in addition to those given in other sections dealing with particular techniques.)

The main types of constructional sheet materials are:

Reinforced thermosetting plastics
Thermoplastics
Stainless steel
Ferrous metals
Non-ferrous metals
Laminates
Composition boards.

Weight-for-weight, reinforced thermosetting plastics sheet (Section Four Part 1) provides the greatest tensile strength and impact resistance. Sheer hardness and resistance to corrosion, temperature variations, etc., is provided by stainless steel. For sheer versatility, the honours go to thermoplastics. **These materials can all be exposed to the normal range of weather conditions in temperate climates, without surface coating of any kind.**

A Glass-fibre reinforced and mass-pigmented polyester resin sheet: 6 feet × 4 feet, coloured. Analysis:

Gelcoat and three laminating coats standard resin	18 lb
Peroxide catalyst at 4% (M.E.K.P.)	12 oz
Accelerator	12 oz
Typical pigment, dispersed in resin	1 lb
Glass Fibre, chopped strand matt at $1\frac{1}{2}$ oz per ft^2	7 lb

(N.B. Allowance made for normal wastage)

This sheet would take about four hours to fabricate, including the waiting period while the gelcoat goes off (at 65° F.). Two instead of three laminations of glass fibre would reduce the weight and cost proportionately, as would the elimination of pigments. F.R.P. sheet can be made by hand lay-up over a flat, clean, sheet of glass, steel, P.V.C., F.R.P. or hard-painted wood, using separating agent.

The back of an F.R.P. sheet can be surfaced with surfacing tissue (fine glass-fibre sheet) using a mohair roller. F.R.P. cutting tools are coping saw, hacksaw blade, power jig-saw with metal cutting blade. Shaping tools are body file, dreadnought file, Surform or Shaper tools, rotary Surform or Shaper tools. Abrasives are production paper (40, 60 or 80 grit), waterproof carborundum paper (150, 220 used wet, 320, 360 and 400 used wet with soap), by hand with an X.P. sanding block, or on a rotary, drum or orbital power sander. Fill countersunk screws in F.R.P. sheet with a resin/glass powder/body filler (see U.K. Buyer's Guide to Section Four).

B Stainless steel sheet is delivered in a wide variety of types, each suited to a particular application. Main types are austenitic, ferritic, martensitic. Normal finish is 'industrial bright', polishing one or both sides adds to cost. Drill at low speeds on a centrepunched marker, using a hardened drill; when the countersunk screw is visible, it can be masked by the use of 'mirror fixing' screws, with tapped heads over which fit caps. 24- or 22-gauge sheet can be cut or trimmed (just above) with shears, but for heavier sheet a pair of nibblers or a heavy guillotine will be needed. Remove smears or marks with domestic metal polish, or with buffing compound and a power polisher.

C The volume cost of rigid P.V.C. as a polymer is very cheap, even in consideration of the relatively high density of the material (88 lb per ft^3), but the consumer must pay also for additives and processing. The cheapest vinyl is the industrial grade, usually grey or black, which has a surface akin to milled steel—the cost of extrusion and lamination just doubles the volume cost of the material as a polymer. The inclusion of opaque pigments and stabilizers and lamination with satin finish both sides raises cost further, and the inclusion of opaque pigments and lamination with polished surfaces both sides raises cost yet again.

High-density polythene has a lower density (lb per ft^3) than vinyl, as does polypropylene, and they are both easier to polish and are reusable. Both materials may therefore be cheaper than vinyl, though their heat-resistant properties do encourage retail price-raising.

In cutting and drilling thermoplastic sheets it is necessary to avoid the generation of heat through friction beyond the softening point of the material: P.V.C.—76° C., high-density polythene—140° C., polymethyl methacrylate (Perspex; Plexiglas or lucite in the U.S.A.)—110° C. This is to say that the cutting action of a drill or saw should be fast and sharp, and the friction contact minimal. Regrind drills to an included angle of 140°, preferably with a drill having a quick spiral (large helix angle). Lubricating oil will help to dissipate heat if drilling a hole through 2 inch-thick rigid P.V.C. for instance, but obviously for this purpose, as with using a power jig-saw, H.D. polythene is more heat resistant. When sawing with a hacksaw, use a relatively large-toothed blade (18 to the inch) to avoid binding. When using cast plastics (polymethyl methacrylate, for example) avoid notching; cracks run very fast through the molecular structure of such materials—it is even possible to divide a heavy P.V.C. sheet accurately by chopping the edge with a knife while the sheet is flexed to produce tension. Woodworking saws can be used on P.V.C.

Non-ferrous metals—copper, zinc, brass, aluminium, etc.—are manufactured in sheet form, but are subject to oxidation and very soft for use as structural members. Copper and brass are relatively expensive, while (for interior use) aluminium sheet and beading is very cheap, and can be purchased with elements added to stiffen the material and cut down oxidation.

The cost of ferrous and non-ferrous sheet metals fluctuates, suffice to say that they are cheap and may be obtained either industrial-finished, satin-finished or polished, at cost per square foot worked on. Where sheet metal is required to retain a degree of industrial finish without deterioration (as in some of the box constructions of American sculptor Donald Judd) the use of galvatite or galvanized sheet is inferior to the use of mild steel which is subsequently sent to an industrial anodizing and galvanizing plant for processing. All metals tend to be delivered with scratches and indentations, and must be inspected before they are used—rolled steel usually turns out to have domed areas which may not be removed (since they are due to uneven stretching), up to 18 gauge, but at 16 gauge or thicker are more likely to be flat. **Where using screws or bolts on sheet metal, avoid the combination of metals, or electrolysis may cause damage in time.** Before attempting to bond ferrous materials to plastics it is advisable to prime the metal with an oxide primer.

Plastics adhesives

All thermoplastics have low-energy characteristics—that is, they do not show signs of electrical, thermal or frictional energy, and are resistant to chemical attack: they are therefore the most difficult substances to bond. No adhesive will provide a joint between plastics comparable with that produced by high-frequency or hot-gas welding (Section Four Part 2). Adhesives are either based on cellulose compounds, or on polyvinyl acetate (P.V.A.). It is vital to ascertain the material to be bonded: chemical resistances of plastics vary enormously, and it is for instance impossible to achieve a good bond between P.V.C. and polypropylene without selecting an adhesive designed to overcome the lower-energy surface of the latter. Between plastics a bond may be achieved if the surfaces are first abraded to provide some mechanical grip, and then degreased with alcohol or ether (the same thing) or even a petroleum degreasing fluid as used in the motor refinishing trade. Apply a thin film of adhesive (see list of suppliers and consult) to both surfaces and allow solvents to evaporate before impacting. This procedure is unlikely to prove satisfactory on polythene or polypropylene surfaces. Polyester resin may be used to form a bond, though this is not recommended by manufacturers, and the grip is largely mechanical, due to the resistance of thermoplastics to the styrene monomer, as witnessed by the ease with which resin may be removed from plastic bowls. Wood should be twice coated with adhesive before impacting. The best adhesives for use on plastics are those based on cellulose compounds, these being highly inflammable. No smoking, the flash point is room temperature. Keep lids sealed.

Interior grade sheets: laminates and composition boards

It is now common practice to use hardboard, which is very cheap for the construction of patterns from which to make plaster or reinforced plastic castings (Sections One and Four). The grades of hardboard obtainable from a particular supplier should be noted when ordering. Cubic and curved surfaces (down to a radius of about 1 foot) may be built up over a light wood frame. Follow straight-cut edges on the sheet rather than trust the softwood used, which will warp before use in all cases. Over curved surfaces provide a well-defined curve on the frame with depth of frame material (never end-grain) to take pins. Tack straight edge of hardboard first, then follow around curve at same rate on each side of curve using pins 1 inch apart. Where the curve is too fast for hardboard, a curve may be incorporated using 22-gauge galvatite or zinc. When tacking hardboard, always use square-section, copper-coated, diamond-headed panel pins. These diminish 'dimples' around tacking. The most efficient method is to make a three-sided female form over an exterior frame, plus a separate fourth side, and to cast these off directly into reinforced plastic. Shellac or polyurethane varnish hardboard, follow up with non-silicone wax and P.V.A. separating agent.

Very rigid laminates are now available, either as all-wood (plywood), wood-plastic (U.K.: Weydec and Arborite and Formica) or metal-foam (aluminium–X.P.) sheets. Advantages claimed for laminates are that they do not warp and have high lateral strength. In fact, plywood does warp considerably, and chipboard, which is manufactured from wood pulp and bonding agents—expands when damp. Blockboard, as its name suggests, is made by laminating a veneer on to blocks of wood. When damp the laminating glues tend to part company, and the blocks burst. Plastic laminates are simply made by the addition of one or two sheets of P.V.C. on to either a chipboard or blockboard sheet. A wide variety of these materials is available (see list of suppliers), at sizes from 4 ft × 4 ft standard up to 8 ft × 4 ft maximum, to a maximum thickness of 1 inch. The plastic colour and texture is limited by current decorator's demands. The basic limitation of such materials, as with foam-sandwich boards, is in each case the same—how to deal with the open section of the material? The obvious answer—to bond a section of the facing material to edges and trim—suffers the drawback that all unstable materials (wood pulp or block and porous foam) need to have room and vents to 'breathe'.

Chipboard and black board are excellent materials on which to use a jig-saw, with grainless chipboard having the edge. They cost little, but any paint surface (Section Nine Part 1, see use of synthetic fillers for maximum flatting of surface) is likely to be ruptured by movement of the unstable material underneath.

Much the strongest of these materials, and recommended for interior-exhibited constructions is plywood. Plywood is laminated from millimetre-thick sheets of veneer, either birch or some other fairly hard wood, glued under pressure. To order, laminates may be moulded over patterns provided by the customer, as in the boat-building industry. The Mosquito (twin-engined fighter-bomber of World War II) was designed to take advantage of the structural properties of ply, and it now forms the hull and deck material for most power boats. See Section Eight for notes on finishing.

Part 2 · Specialized Hand Tools

Many new tools lack proper names, due to their development by commercial firms who understandably do not wish to lose their registered link with the names of such tools. I hope that rival firms will forgive, for instance, the fact that I refer to Surform-type tools as 'Surforms'.

Surform: a range of open-bladed cutting tools, akin to planes, for rough use on plaster, wood and laminates. Serrated cut on plastics.

Metal files: high-tensile steel blades with cross-cut pattern, for use only on metals.

Dreadnought files: blades with curved, forward-facing cutting edges for fast, clean cutting-back of metals and plastics.

Rasps: file-shaped or spatula-shaped blades with teeth punched directly out of the blade, leaving indents behind them; for use on wood only.

Coping saw: a fine, replaceable blade some 8 inches long held under tension by a screw-out handle mounted in a deep metal frame; for use in keyhole cuts on plywood and for trimming plastics.

Hacksaw: a fine, replaceable blade, 10 or 12 inches long, held under tension by a metal frame with a wing-nut adjustment at front; for cutting metals or plastics; various rates of cut per blade type.

Fretsaw: a deeper version of the coping saw, for use on wood: see power jig-saws in Part 3.

Rip saw: a wood-handled saw with an unsupported blade 24 inches or longer. The teeth are deeper and have a greater set than those of the apparently similar crosscut saw common in woodwork shops; for cutting end grain wood.

Tenon saw: a supported blade, having a brass grip along the spine of the fine-toothed blade; for use in cutting wood joints only.

Eclipse saw: an all-alloy saw with various position blade for rough cutting wood, light metal, plaster and plastics (U.K. trade name).

Yankee pump-action driver: various screwdriver bits may be seated at the head of a worm action shank, which converts downward pressure into torque. The only tool for use on large constructions.

Phillips driver: for use on Phillips screws having heads indented with + ; a driver is needed for each size of Phillips screw, despite manufacturer's claims.

Allen keys: fit Allen screws, which are constant-diameter screws with hexagonal socket at one end.

Spokeshave: used extensively by cabinet-makers for freehand planing over curved wood surfaces.

Guillotine: see Buyer's Guide for names of large trade suppliers of metal working equipment such as sheet steel guillotines; these have replaceable blade section bolted to lever arm and can therefore be serviced if bought secondhand through an engineering firm.

Bolt cropper: long-handled, parallel-action cutters with adjustable parts for cutting various thickness of metal rod.

Side-cutting pliers: rather unsatisfactory for wire-cutting, and not as specialized as parallel or self-gripping pliers.

Parallel pliers: with cantilever action for even grip.

Self-gripping pliers: quickly adjustable snap-action pliers which are effectively a portable vice.

Stanley Knife: U.K. trade name for one of a range of razor-sharp blade carrying metal handle sets.

Lino knife: blunt edges to parallel blade, but with an angled or curved cutting edge at end, for general cutting and paring.

Rotary cutter: just a sharp edged washer on a spindle attached to a handle—for even curved cuts in soft materials.

Woodworking vice: clamps to wood bench by means of wing-nut and bolt headed screw; jaws of wood, covered with felt pads. Alternatively, though not as useful to woodcarvers, a metal vice which sits flush with bench-top.

Engineering vice: hardened jaws and (preferably) a quick release handle; jaws come in various widths, and actions are simple box-type or accurate cylindrical fitting.

Adjustable spanner: saves worrying about metric or fractional nut sizes.

G-cramps: from tiny 3-inch cramps up to yard-long woodworker's cramps, with wing-nut tightening adjustment.

Pipe-bender: it is better to cold-bend a pipe in a purpose-built bending tool than to heat it and turn it over in a vice. Interchangeable jaws.

Woodcarving bench clamp: a hole is drilled in the bench, through which a bolt-headed screw fixed from underneath with a wing-nut is passed, securing the clamp. This acts as the fulcrum when one end of the clamp is raised by means of a screw, thus forcing the other down on to the work.

Taps and diecutters: internal or external thread sections which are used to cut screw spirals into metal rod—producing nuts or bolts. These are inexpensively available in sets, note that the cutters are adjustable for initial bite and final cleaning of thread. Work in half-turns, using oil.

Ball pene hammer: hammer with slightly convex face and hemispherical face, for forging and engineering work.

Claw hammer: having a nail-removing claw at rear; for woodworking only.

Twist drill: hand-drill for use with drill bits for putting fine or medium holes accurately through all materials. Replaceable chuck. Note firm distinction between masonry drill bits, hardened steel drill bits and softer wood drill bits, also regrinding angle for plastics.

Brace: behind the chuck the handle performs a crank action, cushioned against the body. For use on woods, with large diameter bits of various types.

Chisel type: cold chisel—for use on concrete; firmer chisel—with bevelled blade for strength and lightness; mortice chisel—with deep, narrow blade for gouging holes and grooves; gouge—with convex blade for woodcarving; stonecarving chisels—Section 5; chasing tools—small and hard, for cleaning burrs from face of bronze and aluminium castings.

Gauging tools: spirit levels, calipers, set squares, engineer's squares, mason's square, plumb bob and line, expanding rule, boxwood and metal rules, hardened steel straight edge, carpenter's bevel.

Part 3 · Power Tools

Two species of power tool exist: the domestic and the industrial. The domestic tool is designed to achieve flexibility at low cost, the industrial tool is heavy-duty, specialized, and more costly both in itself and in the need for extra tools rather than extra accessories. Power tools are generally far cheaper in the U.S.A.

Power drill
The basis of all domestic set-ups. It is not worth going for the industrial power drill—developments have led to low-cost drills at the upper end of the domestic range which offer all the advantages set out below at low

weight. The continental machines are lighter at the time of writing, due to their extensive use of plastic casings. A domestic power drill, to be flexible and fast, should possess most or all of the following features.

A Variable speed. Under 1,000 r.p.m. for drilling steel, over 2,000 r.p.m. for sanding, cutting. Some machines have variable resistance in circuit, which reduces power at low speed: switch change is preferable. 'Skil' offer a unique silicon trigger mechanism which reduces or increases speed according to trigger pressure without affecting torque.

B Powerful, protected electric motor. Check with a demonstrator that the on-load speed of the drill is not affected by more than about 15%. Automatic cut-outs are fitted to some drills, chuck may be gripped in vice and motor triggered without harming windings. Alternative protection is offered by welded armatures. When sparking at two brushes visible inside rear of drill decreases, it is advisable to have new brushes fitted.

C $\frac{3}{8}$-inch chuck. This is an optimum chuck size. Chuck should be removable if range of attachments or a new chuck are to be fitted.

D Double insulation and side handle which will not foul chuck.

Attachments
Paint stirrer—use slow speed, hold can. Screwdriver and Phillips screwdriver. Orbital sander—very useful. Jig-saw—often clumsy, use high speed. Circular saw—dangerous if used with continuous running button depressed, limited depth of cut. Sanding drum—foam-backed drum with loose (usually too loose) belt, very fast cutting. Sanding pad—foam-backed pad which allows some degree of contour sanding without severe swirl marks. Sanding disc—rubber backed, use paper disc until it tears. Polishing pad—a lambswool bonnet on a softish pad, leaves some swirl marks. Grinder—either fitted to wheel arbor or bench set. Wire brush or cup—puts heavy load on drill. Lathe—more of a toy than a tool.

Angle grinder
A heavy duty tool for use in cutting and surface-gouging of heavy castings or welded steel sculpture. Since such a tool must stand up to rough treatment it is advisable to push demonstrator on question of reliability. The motor produces a great deal of torque; check that grips are well placed and insulated to dampen vibration. 'On–off' switch must be easy to reach and positive—always check that it is 'off' before plugging in tool, or torque will lift machine out of your hands or off the bench. Cutters take the form of epoxy resin/glass fibre/aluminium oxide disc: the law requires that an efficient guard be fitted when using cutter. Should the cutting wheel distintegrate without guard in place, the user will be disembowelled. Solid grinding wheels are used for flat work.

Power plane
Not warranted unless constantly required, as cost is high. Very efficient machine which allows even lowering of surface to predetermined depth.

Power jig-saw

Most professional sculptors seem to find very small jig-saws satisfactory. Where it is likely that a machine will be used to make long cuts in thick wood, plywood, plastics, sheet metal—and also to make keyhole cuts with small radius, it is worth considering a larger tool. It has been found that the Stanley Sabre Saw with a heavy-duty motor and tilt base is a cutter which will take a very wide range of blades, make fast clean cuts at all angles through most materials and will do this in a manageable way: most other jig-saws seem rather cumbersome, switches difficult to operate, etc., after the Sabre. However, it is expensive. The large cut-out panels of 1965–6 by Roy Ascot required the use of a larger machine yet, operating on a different principle: the blade here is either a small chisel or a small saw, and reciprocates at over 3,000 r.p.m. The machine has a large foot, allowing it to move freely over the work surface while vibrating, and the blade reciprocates in a guide which can rotate freely through 360° in a horizontal plane, as can the drive mechanism. The operator can get hold of the saw by the fingertips at either side of the blade, and simply push or pull the blade in any direction to make cuts with a radius of anything down to the width of the blade—$\frac{1}{4}$ inch. This type of cutter also allows cuts to be restricted in depth.

Circular saw

A rip or crosscut saw will handle most woodcutting jobs quickly and cleanly, so that it is not worth using a circular saw which cannot cope with jobs obviously beyond the range of a hand tool. This means, for instance, slicing a 2-inch plank in half along the grain—at any angle between 45° and vertical. To make a $2\frac{1}{2}$-inch-deep cut while upright, the saw must have a 7-inch blade; such a blade puts enormous strain on the motor and really demands that the machine be of the heavy-duty type. Portable saws are not legally convertible for bench work, and therefore have no bench-fixing lugs or constant-running switch. Blades will be blunt after two days continuous use, and will have to be sharpened at your toolstore. It is essential that the blade is kept from twisting in the cut, as the strain and friction will de-temper the blade and threaten the motor windings.

Router

A very expensive industrial woodworking tool for gouging accurate grooves.

Belt sander

Useful tool for sculptors working exclusively in metal, allows fast finishing as tough sanding belt passes over flat steel shoe. Portable or bench models.

Orbital sander

More sophisticated and far more effective than rotary sanding devices, the machine puts a long, wide shoe, carrying any kind of wet or dry sanding cloth or paper, through a fast, flat $\frac{3}{16}$-inch orbit. Essentially a portable machine, and perhaps the only way to cut a surface down flat both before and in between painting or polishing operations. Purpose-built sanders orbit much faster than attachments. Compressed air-driven sanders are available for use 45–60 p.s.i.

Nail gun
Not really a power tool, since the motor is added to the gun each time it is used
But this type of cartridge-operated gun will drive special nails and bolts well
home into castings, brickwork, etc., with minimum of effort.

Compressors (Section Nine)

Rivet gun
Aside from the impracticably large rivet guns used in industry, there are some
small hand-operated guns which will expand a soft rivet from one side of the
plate so as to provide an effective joint in light gauge metals. Especially
useful when making light constructions in aluminium, where welding and
brazing can be difficult or expensive, and other means of jointing impracticable

Rotary grinder on flexible drive
Essential where large welded steel sculpture must be ground and polished
This type of machine has a large remote electric motor, drive being transferred
by an armoured flexible cable to a chuck, usually fitted with side handles. The
handles are advisable, as the larger motor allowed by remote drive arrangement
gives high torque and creates danger and fatigue where grip is difficult. This
type of machine is quite distinct in operation from the angle grinder.

Part 4 · Personal Protective Equipment

These notes are intended to service other sections and deal with various types
of protective clothing and equipment.

General
Any protective equipment that is purchased, especially when provided by a
commercial firm or art school, gets left on the shelf more and more as the
users gain confidence and the equipment is found to hamper the work in
progress. It is probably better therefore to err on the side of ease than safety,
and thus increase the likelihood of some sort of protection at all times.

Eyes
Eye protection falls into three distinct categories:

A Lenses to provide protection against particles and dust. These are available
as lightweight spectacle frame-mountings, full-weight goggles and also in
the form of face-shields. The spectacle frame-mountings are the best for
use when carving stone: this is a matter of comfort and ease—it may be
that any heavier protection would simply not be used because of the discomfort. The lenses should be of the type tested by having a steel ball
dropped on them—high impact-resistance minimizes the likelihood of hav-

ing the lens shattered in front of the eye and itself becoming a projectile. For angle and rotary grinding it is also necessary to provide for impact-resistant eye protection, but of a heavier type, and with side cover to prevent ricochet or hot dust from reaching the eye. The goggle type is here the best, and if possible one with breathing holes to lower moisture level in goggles, and also with hard plastic lenses—these are low-energy, do not pick up dust or allow adhesion of spatter. Foundry work allows heavier protection, and requires wider cover with wide-angle vision: use a face-shield of the type which has a visor which can be lifted out of the way. Essential to wear such a visor when pouring molten metal.

B Glare protection. Flame-welding produces intense light which will leach pigments on the retina at an unnaturally fast rate if no protection is given to the eye. Also there is the constant emission of fine debris from the area of the weld. When cutting with the gas torch, larger pieces of red hot steel are likely to be projected at the eye at a high rate when it is close to the work. Frankly it is best to wear the simplest type of goggle for welding—some have flip-up anti-glare lenses which allow clear vision through impact resistant glass, some have one large area of glare and impact resistant glass, but none are as light and easily maintained as the adjustable welder's goggle with impact-resistant plastic lenses in front of glare-eliminating glass.

C High intensity infra-red and ultra-violet ray protection. Normal goggles are quite useless for protection against the rays generated in an electric arc, and the reflection of such rays from the side of the welder is dangerous, also there is the danger of exposing the facial skin tissues to constant radiation. Visor-type and hand-held shield-type masks are made in one piece of reinforced plastic, into which 99·5% efficient filters are fitted. The visor type has a headband which may induce discomfort and headaches, and is difficult to swing in and out of place (necessary, since the lens is op-aque until the work area is lit by arc), added to which it is unnecessary where no other operators are working than yourself. Note that different filters are needed for different types of electrode and plant, and that **glare-protective goggles are quite ineffective against these rays.** The lens or filter is itself protected with an impact-resistant glass or plastic lens, which will be replaceable at low cost.

Hands

Gloves to prevent hands from becoming raw through handling of rusty steel and stone blocks need to be very short and wide—if not, they are difficult to get on and off quickly and tend not to be used. Gloves are available for this kind of use with rubber grips on the palms. When using synthetic resins the main purpose in wearing gloves (other than for persons suffering from dermatitis) is to cut down time spent washing. Heavy neoprene or rubber gloves are un-necessary and expensive, so that the best and cheapest protection is probably offered by disposable polythene gloves. Barrier creams are an alternative, but must be very effective to facilitate effortless removal of gelled resin mixed with glass fibre. Foundry work and welding call for a compromise between a manageable glove and a fully protective gauntlet: both are available in as-bestos and in chrome-tanned leather.

Dusts and vapours

There is a basic difference between toxic and non-toxic dusts and vapours, and between filters for dusts on the one hand and vapours on the other. It is common to see light smog-type masks used as if they provided a sort of blanket cover for this kind of hazard, which they do not. **The major danger in the field of sculpture at this time exists in the form of non-toxic dusts**—that is, dusts which offer no immediate hazard to the person who breathes them, but which will not be dissolved by the solvents in the lungs, and can form the basis of a cumulative irritant which encourages a growth of lung-blocking substances ultimately resulting in silicosis. Stonecarvers need not really worry about this hazard unless they spend all day and every day hammering away at lumps of granite. Metal powders probably offer a greater risk than the majority of stones. The most dangerous irritant at this time is one of the most common—a mixture of powdered synthetic resin and powdered glass pouring off power-sanded reinforced plastics, and certainly for this last case it is necessary to health rather than comfort to wear an efficient mask. Filters for pneumoconiosis producing dusts are available now as simple corrugated pads, but if other types of mask are also needed, as will almost certainly be the case, it is as well to buy a rubber dust mask with an interchangeable and replaceable filter section, fitting it in this instance with a recommended filter for fine dusts. Check the return valve regularly. Last come the organic vapours, produced in synthetic resin application and spray painting. Only in the case of lead-based paints, which are not recommended, are these vapours likely to prove toxic, but all may cause discomfort, and cellulose paints will irritate the lungs and breathing passages with solvents. Use a standard filter for organic vapours, dust filters will let all the important irritants through, leaving the harmless contents to clog the mask.

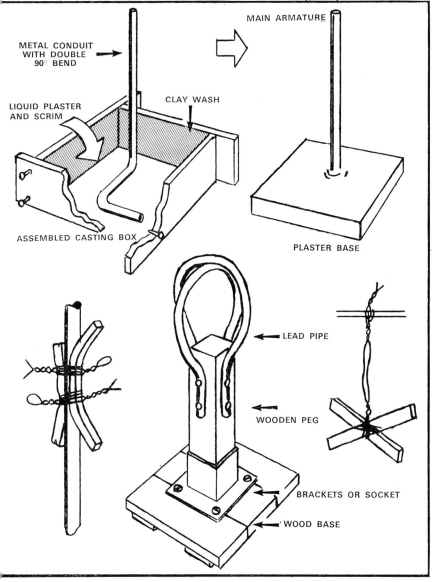

METAL CONDUIT WITH DOUBLE 90° BEND

MAIN ARMATURE

LIQUID PLASTER AND SCRIM

CLAY WASH

ASSEMBLED CASTING BOX

PLASTER BASE

LEAD PIPE

WOODEN PEG

BRACKETS OR SOCKET

WOOD BASE

Fig 21

Armature construction

At top: a steel support for a direct plaster model, sunk in plaster base. *Below, left to right:* a method of double tightening wire fastenings to secure soft aluminium or wood to main support for complex clay armature; a head portrait support; a butterfly, which hangs and supports clay in bulk.

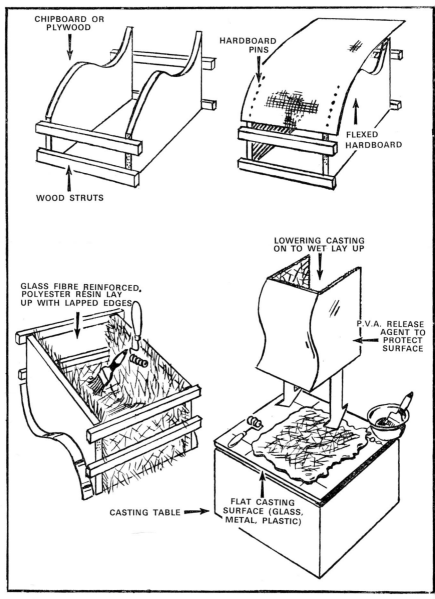

Fig 22

Mould construction
Example of common method, producing a regular form by constructing as negative (the rough hardboard face and frame are on the outside)—before treatment with shellac and P.V.A. Form is cast in synthetic resin (Section Four). Fill in missing faces by lowering casting on to wet lay up on flat surface.

Fig 23

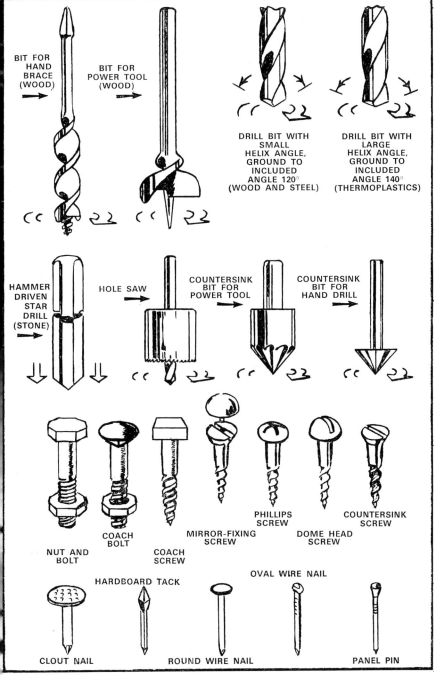

BIT FOR HAND BRACE (WOOD)

BIT FOR POWER TOOL (WOOD)

DRILL BIT WITH SMALL HELIX ANGLE, GROUND TO INCLUDED ANGLE 120° (WOOD AND STEEL)

DRILL BIT WITH LARGE HELIX ANGLE, GROUND TO INCLUDED ANGLE 140° (THERMOPLASTICS)

HAMMER DRIVEN STAR DRILL (STONE)

HOLE SAW

COUNTERSINK BIT FOR POWER TOOL

COUNTERSINK BIT FOR HAND DRILL

NUT AND BOLT

COACH BOLT

COACH SCREW

MIRROR-FIXING SCREW

PHILLIPS SCREW

DOME HEAD SCREW

COUNTERSINK SCREW

CLOUT NAIL

HARDBOARD TACK

ROUND WIRE NAIL

OVAL WIRE NAIL

PANEL PIN

H

U.K. Buyer's Guide to Section Seven (U.S. readers refer to p. 8)
Unless otherwise stated, addresses are London: branches in addition to London are in brackets.

Aluminium sheet
      Local stockists
      Alcob Metals Ltd
      London Metal Warehouses Ltd
      Non-Ferrous Stockholders Ltd

Stainless steel stockists—Buyer's Guide to Section Three

Synthetic resins and glass fibre—Buyer's Guide to Section Four

Plywood and chipboard distributors
      C. F. Anderson & Sons Ltd
      T. Brewer & Co. Ltd
      Y. Goldberg & Sons Ltd
      Local timber merchants

Plastic laminate manufacturers
      Local building trade stockists
      Bakelite Ltd. 'Warerite'
      B.X. Plastics Ltd, Essex
      Formica Ltd. 'Formica'
      Arborite Company (U.K.) Ltd. 'Arborite'

Printing (specialists in screen printing on P.V.C.)
      Pan Screen Printers, Yorkshire

General Tools, Ironmongery and Engineering Accessories

Armature construction materials
      Local engineering suppliers, stockists of ferrous and non-ferrous metal rod; secondhand electrical conduit from contractors

Hand tools
      Local woodworking and metalworking tool suppliers

Heavy grinding equipment
      A.E.G. Ltd
      Bosch Ltd
      Langham Tools Co.

Ironmongery—nuts, bolts, screws, etc.
      Buck & Ryan Ltd
      Nettlefold & Moser Ltd

Power tools
       Black & Decker Ltd
       Scintilla Ltd. 'Lesto'
       Skill Ltd
       Stanley Bridges Ltd
       Super Tool Co. (1951) Ltd. 'Cutawl' H/D jig-saws
       Wolf Ltd

Pneumatic tools—Buyer's Guide to Section Five

Timber
       Local timber merchants, moulding suppliers

Rigid plastic sheet—Buyer's Guide to Section Four

Protective clothing and equipment
       British American Optical Co., Hertfordshire
       Minnesota Mining and Manufacturing Co. '3M'
       Northide Ltd, Cheshire

Part 1 · Wood and Plaster (including priming and gilding)
Part 2 · Metals—Anodizing and Electroplating

Part 1 · Wood and Plaster

As noted in Section One, plaster surfaces cannot be smoothed efficiently until dry, even when using waterproof carborundum paper. This is because there is a likelihood of pulling the 'green' or cheesy surface of the material away, rather than abrading it off. If the surface of the plaster is made up of many superimposed layers and additions of plaster, there will be a tendency to 'shucking'. When plaster is being smoothed, it can be assumed that it is to be sealed (with shellac or polyurethane varnish) and therefore, since it will need to be dry before painting, it is best to use glasspaper and an X.P. sanding block. Where the plaster is being worked to a smooth polish in an isolated area only, during general forming, use wet and dry paper with plenty of water.

If a sanded plaster mould or positive surface needs filling, shellac it first, and then cast from it—removing the holes as promontories from the positive or negative result. **Do not attempt to fill dry plaster with fresh plaster.**

Carved wood
Use a wood block and either glasspaper of successively finer grades or the three grades of production paper available. Production paper is much tougher, but much coarser also, than glasspaper. An X.P. block will help even sanding of curved surfaces. See also 'Polishing'.

Priming
If a plaster form is to be moulded, it should be varnished with shellac or polyurethane. Shellacked lightly once every 10 minutes, the form should be shiny after three or four coats. If not, and it is necessary to avoid the green and yellow discoloration attendant on plaster surfaces, first give a coat of *Dulux* Plaster and Asbestos Primer/Sealer, which is very thin and efficient at reducing porosity, and then one or two coats of white emulsion. The emulsion paint, when dry, can be brushed to a polish. Any filling can be done with *Polyfilla* (cellulose filler paste).

Plywood, chipboard and hardwood constructions can all be worked with power tools (Section Seven Part 3), particularly drum, disc and orbital sanders. Reduce the roughness of the surface as much as possible on flat sheets, but leave some key for a coat of either pink wood primer, a direct undercoat, or a synthetic primer/filler. Any large cracks or indentations can be filled with plastic wood, or a resin-bonded filler (body fillers). If the surface is not to be painted, various grades and colours in stopping paste are obtainable. Holes can be filled with sawdust and casein resin glue. The best filler to use over pink wood primer is an oilbound filler at knifing consistency. Note that all stoppers and fillers sink—leaving indents over C/S screws. The strongest method of filling such holes, and of building up wide cracks or edges, is in thin layers of plastic wood or wood stopping, each allowed to dry hard, the last being set proud.

Polishing
Where a previously painted surface is to be polished, use paint stripper in quantity over small areas, constantly agitating. This is preferable to leaving the

tripper to soak through the paint and into the wood, and allows constant
attention. Scrubbing with hot water will clean and bleach wood, but softens
the fibres permanently at the surface. Knots or holes may be drilled or reamed
out and plugged tight with a standard thickness dowel in the appropriate
grade of wood, using casein resin glue. Finish sanding with 'flour' paper
(green in colour). There is no way of getting oil out of timber, and thus no way
of polishing such wood.

The clean wood can either be given a penetrating or superficial treatment—
oiling or polishing, both of which achieve substantially the same result: to
make the natural colour of the wood more visible. Light is normally reflected
from the surface dust and fibrous nap of the wood in random patterns. In
making this surface transparent, much the same effect is achieved as when
a glass-bottomed box is lowered through the reflective surface of water. If
a deep but non-greasy and rather soft colour is wanted, oil the wood, using
refined linseed. Any treatment advised by a specialist to prevent worm is
best undertaken before oiling or other treatment.

Polishing can be single or double-staged. Single-stage polishing consists
simply in giving the wood a coat of pure beeswax, softened if necessary by
the addition of turpentine while heated. This wax will penetrate slightly into
the fibres, but when hard will give a soft gloss. Provides some protection
against dirt. Rather greasy in appearance on some woods. Double-stage
polishing begins with an application of one or two fine coats of refined
shellac (white polish), thinned if necessary with methylated spirit (alcohol).
While polishing it may assist the build-up of a gloss to soak some cotton wool
in white polish and wrap some soft cloth around it—using it as a bunched
pad to burnish the surface. Follow when hard with beeswax to achieve a hard
gloss which is highly protective. A rather brilliant gloss. Bleach wood with
oxalic acid.

Gilding

Can take place over any stable, non-porous surface. A coat of flat red oil
paint is recommended over any surface to be gold-leafed, while a white or blue
is suitable for use under silver. Tools required are razor blades, flat camel-hair
mops, bushy sable mops. Materials are gold or silver leaf, in books; Japan gold
size.

It is vital to work in a still atmosphere. Clean and paint surface, let it dry
thoroughly. Dust off with paintbrush. Open book and hold down loose-leaves
of gold with mop to decide area which is to be covered at a time: books are
made which have gold or silver stuck lightly to interleaved tissues, which makes
life easier. Use a small clean sable to paint one area thinly with Japan gold
size. This size contains rapid driers and must be applied deliberately in one go;
watch the size and test from time to time with outside of little finger until
surface is tacky but does not come off. Lift loose leaf by pressing flat mop and
inverting—slow movements are essential—and lay to work surface. Very gently
stipple over surface with bushy sable mop. Later bone down using tissue
between tool and gilt. Cracking of gold and silver is difficult to avoid entirely,
but will be acceptable over a suitably painted ground. Transfer-type sheets are
said to work and bushy mop is used to stipple through tissue—do not lift

tissue away until all the gold or silver has been deposited. Complex areas may be covered by holding the leaf with the edge of a razor blade while a section is lifted free with the flat mop.

Part 2 · Metals

Anodizing and electroplating
Bright metal surfaces, such as polished stainless steel and the precious metals are fairly stable, even where they tarnish. But most cheaper ferrous and non-ferrous metals are attacked very rapidly by the atmosphere, particularly in heavily polluted areas. Electrolysis provides a means of treating metals so as to give them a degree of corrosion-resistance, and of changing their appearance. A person with 35 years experience of lecturing and practising in electrolysis has warned me that the exact nature of the electrochemical processes involved is still a bit of a mystery, so that definitions could be misleading. The following is a gloss on those problems you must discuss with an electroplating jobber.

Electrolysis
The term refers to any application of the principal of passing an electric current between two electrodes (the anode and the cathode) through an electrolyte. Water can thus be separated into hydrogen, and a car battery will deliver electricity, aluminium can be oxidized, and cadmium deposited over steel, all within the same kind of process.

Anodizing
'Anodizing' has become accepted as the term for passivation treatment of aluminium, though certain other metals are susceptible. As suggested by the term anodizing, the aluminium is made to form the anode (positive electrode) when submerged in the electrolyte. 'Passivation' refers to the chemical change brought about at the metal surface, which anticipates and nullifies further oxidation. The process is completed when the surface is sealed by 'absorption' (a filling-in of pores in the anodized metal surface).

The anodized aluminium may be treated with one of a large range of colour-fast dyes before sealing; these dyes will withstand atmospheric attack for long periods. In heavily polluted areas (without smokeless zones), there may be discoloration, also treatment with strong detergents will affect the dyes.

The high porosity of castings makes them difficult to treat with an industrial anodized finish, though anodizing will certainly 'take' on these surfaces: it is necessary to take special account of irregularities in the material, such as welded joints. The process is very cheap, and local jobbing firms will quote for 'one–off' treatments, advising also on preparation.

Electroplating
Here the ionization of an electrode (the charged electrode sheds positive

ions to the negative electrode) causes its physical decomposition, and electrodeposition on the other electrode. The exchange is perfectly controlled, so that an anode of chromium (or of cadmium, nickel, copper, zinc, etc.) is transferred evenly on to the prepared surface of the cathode (the metal or metallized object to be plated).

Range of applications

A completely sealed surface which can be treated with metallic powder will form sufficient basis for electroplating. It is therefore possible to treat a plaster cast so that it is completely non-porous, and then dust with graphite powder or bronze powder, or to do this to wood. To prevent absorption of the electrolyte during plating absolutely, the object may either be saturated in heated oil or wax (a cumbersome but effective method of sealing and of lowering buoyancy), or it may be surfaced with shellac or polyurethane varnish (problems will arise in keeping the object submerged in the electrolyte). The sealed surface is then dusted evenly with graphite powder or bronze powder (if it does not want to stick, begin by painting water and graphite on to the surface).

Electro-adhesive coatings have been developed to facilitate deposits on low-energy plastic surfaces (e.g. 'A.B.S.'—acrylonitrile butadiene styrene) and other non-conductive substances, so that the range of plating applications has increased. But the very special nature of the problems involved make it necessary for the reader to refer cases to a plating specialist.

Metal surfaces must be brought to a degree of finish that requires a lot of hard and efficient work. Consult a plating specialist, and get him to show you the kind of surface he wishes to work on. Chrome plate is like cellulose paint— it does not lay a soft glossy skin over the surface, but lays accurately and very thinly into scratches and over dust. Large or very flat surfaces are not welcome in a plating shop, as irregularities and dust-blemishes are difficult to avoid, and on a mirror surface they are unmistable.

Buyer's guide

Note that most firms in the electroplating business find that trial runs, preparation of electrolytes, etc., require that a run of work be undertaken to maintain economy. It will be necessary to do a systematic search through the Trades Directory to find a 'jobber'. Cost is very high.

Alloy castings for external weathering

Pure aluminium is not only more malleable than aluminium alloys (so that accidental distortions in casting may be corrected) but also weathers very well. L.M.6. (aluminium with a 10–13% silicon content) is easier to manage in casting stages, is harder than pure metal, also weathers quite well.

Natural weathering of aluminium produces a pale grey powder, which forms a self-protecting patina. Darkening can be effected by smoking casting with carbon deposit from pure acetylene flame—but the casting must be preheated. This deposit can then be secured for about two years weathering by brushing in a silicone wax, heating again and brushing up. Easy to re-treat a casting darkened in this way.

Aluminium can be cleaned with a very dilute solution of potash; wash with warm water and dry off.

Clean bronze by dipping in equal quantities of nitric and sulphuric acid dispersed in 40 parts (by volume) of water, plus one-fifth the quantity of acid (by weight) in salt: leave overnight. Wash off with water and dry. Bronze can be cleaned more quickly by fast dipping in 100 parts nitric acid, one part salt, one part calcinated soot: wash in water after seconds.

Buyer's Guide to Section Eight (U.S. readers refer to p. 8)
Unless otherwise stated, addresses are London: branches in addition to London are in brackets.

Gilding materials
        Lechertier Barbe Ltd
        Alec Tiranti Ltd
        Varnish Industries Ltd

Abrasives (cloths, papers, waterproof papers, pastes and wheels)
        The Carborundum Co. Ltd
        Grinding Improvements (Edinburgh) Ltd, Surrey
        John Oakey & Sons Ltd
        Minnesota Mining & Manufacturing Co. Ltd. '3M'
        Universal Grinding Wheel Co. Ltd
        Motor refinishing trade factors

Polishing and buffing equipment, mops, wheels, etc.
        W. Canning & Co. Ltd (Glasgow, Birmingham)
        Cruickshanks Division of Forestal Industries (U.K.) Ltd
        Speed Surfaces Ltd. (Granite)

Anodizing and metal colouring services
        Aluminium & Alzac Ltd (Birmingham)
        Renu Metal Finishing (1960) Ltd
        Woodmet Ltd, Cheshire

Electroplating services (chrome, etc.)
        W. Horwood & Sons Ltd
        Metro Engineering & Plating Works Ltd, Middlesex
        The Midland Electroplating Co., Nottingham
        W. Sanders & Son Ltd

Sandblasting services
        H. G. Sommerfield Ltd

Protective clothing—Buyer's Guide to Section Seven

Part 1 · Paint Technology

This is a very complex field, covered in extraordinary detail in standard works by paint chemists. The basic question is: just what is the paint required to do in a particular case?

A To colour a surface
B To protect a surface from exposure or chemical attack
C To provide a key for subsequent paint
D To form an interface between chemically incompatible surfaces
E To make a colour more visible and protect a paint surface
F To texture or de-texture a surface

The media readily available to perform in one or more of those ways are:

I Oil paints. Medium: oil; thinners: turpentine substitute. They
(A, B, F) contain extenders, which eke out the expensive pigments used, driers to make the paint go hard quickly, anti-skinning agents to prevent premature oxidation of paint surface, and, generally, stabilizers to prevent separation of the medium, solvents and pigments. Many also contain aluminium stearate or similar substance to render paint thixotropic (non-drip). Cheap oil paint means more extenders and less pigment, less finely ground. Metallic particles are difficult to stabilize, require frequent agitation. Available in matt, eggshell and high gloss finishes, all moderately hard, all of which may be brushed or sprayed over suitable undercoat, or undercoat and primer. Oil primers facilitate sticking to surfaces, undercoats are cheap paints used to reduce porosity. Avoid colour cards biased towards 'pastel shades', as these are likely to be very extended paints, and try also to avoid the use of lead paints, either for undercoating or topcoating. Lead poisoning can be cumulative, small quantities entering through the skin, digestive and repiratory systems. If you make paint, or accelerate proprietary brands with paint driers, note that common driers are poisonous. When applying, use minimum of thinners for maximum gloss and quick drying. Never use turpentine oil for thinning paint. 4–6 hours drying, overnight hard.

II Bituminous. Medium: bitumen; thinner: turpentine substitute.
(B) Bituminous black is really just a cheap and relatively efficient means of preventing rust, or damp-proofing. When applying to steel (where *Brunswick* black is recommended), it may help speed up the operation to heat the metal before painting, as this will throw off the solvents and dry the paint. Ruins brushes. Also available are various rubberized paints, and oil paints containing metallic particles (aluminium), which are good for general protection. Overnight drying.

III Emulsions. Medium: high polymer in colloidal suspension;
(A, B, F) thinners: water. They contain extenders (as oil paints), and very

often a thixotropic agent for non-drip application. Emulsion paints are based on a plastic medium and an emulsion which makes them water-soluble. When the emulsion has dried out they are water-resistant, brushes should therefore be kept wet or washed soon after use. May be used to keep a plaster sculpture from going yellow or getting dusty: thin 30% with water and brush thinly over surface to reduce porosity, then spray a 10% thinned topcoat or brush at full strength—this surface can later be brushed up to a dull shine. Can be used as a cheap undercoat for oilbound paints over wood and plaster. 2 hours drying.

IV Polyurethane paints. Medium: plastic (Urethane); thinners:
(A, B, E, F) turpentine substitute. These paints and varnishes are based on plastics materials, so that you can have expanded polyurethane (foam) and so on. Being a plastic, polyurethane is very strong, and will resist scratching and exposure to a far greater extent than oilbound paints. Also, the hardening process can be much more positive, especially where a two-pack polyurethane paint is used—which is much like a thermosetting resin. Very tough paints (such as those used on ocean-going propellor blades) are necessarily rather crude in finish and colour, and it is better to use one of the standard exterior grade polyurethanes (e.g. 'Kingston Diamond'—U.K.; 'Verathane'—U.S.A.), which contain good pigments and few extenders, and protect them with polyurethane varnish, which is very tough. Quite easy to apply by brushing, though these paints and varnishes are best sprayed, using little or no thinners. Note that it is necessary to achieve a wet gloss with a varnish, but that the varnish may tend to yellow by 2–3% on application, which is especially noticeable over white, grey and pale blue. Brush one coat heavily enough to lose streaks, spray two fine coats thickly enough to float a gloss. Lacking cheap extenders, polyurethanes give brilliant colours, which mix cleanly. Drying time 4–6 hours, but not hard for about 48 hours. For a high gloss, well flat using 360 wet and dry carborundum paper, soap and water, 12 hours after application, before applying finishing coat. Dry for 48 hours before varnishing as a minimum, test varnish to avoid chance of runs or sagging. Paints and varnishes available high gloss, and varnish only as matt finish. Metallic polyurethanes are not available. Varnishes are 12-hour drying, 72-hours hard.

V Synthetics. Medium: high polymer dissolved in hydrocarbons;
(A, B, C, thinners: pure American turpentine or as directly recommended
D, F) by supplier/manufacturer. Synthetics are based on plastics materials, and are very hard wearing. Mainly used in the motor trade, as an alternative to cellulose for painting commercial vehicles. Synthetic paints can be obtained in 'lines', that is, as a series: primer (for wood, for metal, for plastics and so on), filler, undercoat, topcoat, each with either a brushing or spraying-consistency thinners. Spray thinners dry faster, giving a dust-

free surface in twenty minutes. Only available through motor trade suppliers, these paints are excellent as primer/fillers, and give a very good, cheap finish. When hard, synthetics are not attacked by the solvents in cellulose paints, and are therefore used as build-up coats in the cellulose process. Available in matt and high gloss finishes. Over metal surfaces use zinc oxide synthetic primer, follow with synthetic air drying filler. Over plastics castings (Section Four Part 1) it is necessary to use only the air-drying synthetic filler, which can be brushed or sprayed in thick, easily rubbed-down coats. Synthetic filler paints key well on to plastics, though a self-etching primer can be used for maximum adhesion, and does not soften the laminate. Two hours drying (8 hours for air-drying filler), overnight hardening.

VI (A, B, E) Cellulose paints. Medium: cellulosics; thinners: manufactured to suit various grades of paint, various temperature conditions. Cellulose paints are plastics containing petroleum solvents in quantities, which were developed to take advantage of paint-spraying as a process. The paints are mixed with 20–70% petroleum thinners for use, and are then so fast drying that it is possible in the summer to spray with one hand and touch the dry surface with the other: cannot be brushed. Very expensive, but harder than other paints, and available in a vast range of colours. Cellulose paints are available for air and stove-drying, matt finishes are available for some paints (such as black)—but the majority are gloss finish. A wide range of metallic lacquers, thinned with mist coat thinners. **It is necessary to hold a petroleum licence if you wish to hold stocks of cellulose, failure to do so can lead to prosecution.** These are U.K. regulations:

Do not have more than 3 gallons of cellulose materials on the premises at one time. Store the paint and the thinners in one pint containers, marked: 'Petroleum mixture, giving off inflammable vapours'. Otherwise you fall under the terms of the Petroleum Licencing Act, and will have to spend several hundred pounds on fireproofing and extraction, subject to frequent inspection. The flash point of cellulose is well below the temperature of a studio comfortable to work in, and must be treated as explosive: store away from fires, have a small CO_2 extinguisher or a large foam extinguisher at hand, do not smoke while using, and keep all lids on and tight except when pouring. Notes on extraction under Part 2: spray painting.

Dust-dry in seconds, repaintable in 20 minutes, may be rubbed down in one hour, final coat may be cut down and polished after overnight drying. Varnishes and metallic lacquers are sprayed with 70% mist coat thinners, cutting paste should not be used—Silvo or Brasso and Al car polish is all that can be used without shearing the paint—allow to harden for a week before polishing.

General notes

Cellulose paints will attack oilbound paints and lift them, and will also soften a polyester resin lamination. Synthetic paints are not subject to attack by cellulose, and key well on to most surfaces—therefore provide a barrier coat if required. Various lacquers are available for painting and varnishing where the medium is not stated on the tin—it may be assumed that such paints are thinned with turps and are vulnerable to cellulose. The best varnishes are polyurethane and cellulose, use the former over oilbound and polyurethane paints, the latter over synthetic or mixed into cellulose paints. For keying on to difficult surfaces there are special primer paints:

Aluminium: use a zinc chromate primer, which is a rubbery-looking paint, rather difficult to rub down. It is thought that even this is unsatisfactory, as oxidation may continue, due to electrolysis at the metal surface.

Thermoplastics: use a synthetic self-etching primer, which physically bites a key into the essentially low-energy (low friction, electrical and heat conduction and also chemically inert) surface. Even this is unlikely to hold on to P.T.F.E. (which is used on the Parker 51 to repel ink). Alternative exists in specially made plastic lacquers.

Dry plaster, softboards, asbestos: use domestic brand of asbestos sealer paint.

These notes give only a superficial guide to an enormous subject: further information may be obtained from the detailed literature on the subject.

Part 2 · Brush and Spray Painting

Brush Painting

Section Seven deals with the finishing of the various materials formed by the processes described elsewhere in the text—if the preparation of the surface has been carried out so as to leave it with a smooth, even surface (if a flat or gloss finish is required), and/or with a key for the paint to adhere to (either a primer paint, an undercoat, or just some sealer coat to cut down porosity), there will be little difficulty in painting it. But it is rarely that this has been achieved simply because it is difficult to see very porous areas before they are painted and it is very difficult to see or feel holes and indents in a surface before it has been given a gloss. Therefore aim to apply two well brushed-out thinnish coats rubbing down in between (if on a plane surface), rather than one thick one.

Brushes

The local supplier of paints and tools to the decorating trade will sell good quality brushes (without the flashy handles) at fairly high cost. You pay for something real, in that the finer and longer the bristles, the more you get, and the more paint they will hold at a time. Secondly, it is the case that a cheap brush represents about two uses, if any sort of finish is required, before the bristles splay, wilt and fall out. Use at least three normal brushes, $\frac{1}{2}$-inch,

1-inch, 2-inch and three thin, angled hogshair brushes for lining. The latter make it easier to reach into corners and to pick off hairs dropped by a standard brush, and also are stiffer for painting up to a taped line.

Usage

Load the brush only half-way up the bristles—but load it. Transfer the load directly to the work, and brush out with as few strokes as possible. The alternative is that the brush is submerged, which fills the bristleholder with paint which goes hard, splays the bristles and rots the glue. Then it is squeezed against the can, which removes most of the paint and forces more into the bristle-holder, also running paint down the outside of the can, after which what is left is spread over a small area, which makes the paint too thick and slow drying. Finally, the paint is brushed and brushed until all the solvents are dispersed, which upsets the floating of the gloss!

When you are looking for brushes to paint on glues, polyesters and shellac, it is difficult to resist taking the first one that comes to hand, but it is possible now to buy very cheap brushes for cheap work by the dozen. The good brushes will not survive one night in turps, or even one rinse. They simply have to be emptied of paint with thinners, and then washed out with soap and water, and then dried (one reason why it is quicker to spray it on with an aerosol—if you can afford it). In the U.K. the most practical answer is 'Polyclens', followed by a swill with water—this emulsifier is water-soluble so that the washing really does get out the paint that has been softened, which never really happens when you use turps.

The point is to get the best-quality paint over the largest area as evenly as possible with the least agitation in the shortest time, and then to rescue the brush.

Aerosols

These cost a small fortune, but are worth it for a small job. You simply have to run a test—shake the can until your teeth rattle to get the pressure up and the solvents mixed in, and then find out how much you can get on without runs. Use as described below for spray guns. Invert and fire to clear nozzle.

Spray painting

The hire of spray equipment has been cut down by the cost of cleaning-out clogged lines and guns, but plant can still be hired for a small deposit: look under Plant Hire in the Trades Directory.

There is no special advantage to a sprayed surface, the only gain is in speed. I shall deal mainly with plant capable of a full range of operations, and the reader can decide which of the facilities offered by such plant can be dispensed with. There are two main types of spray painting equipment:

A Low-pressure spraying. A small turbine provides a large volume of air at low pressure, which is slightly heated. This type of plant is recommended as likely to be useful for spray painting sculpture, and for generating air used for hot-gas welding and thermoforming plastics. It is rather cheaper than high-pressure spraying, though largely untested. Volume of air: 70

c.f.m. (cubic feet per minute), pressure of air : 5–10 p.s.i. (lb per in²). Weight and cost of plant are both low—a 30-lb unit can be carried on the back.
B High-pressure spraying. A compressor pumps air out at 40–80 p.s.i., which is unheated. This is the traditional type of plant, recommended by the fact that it is well documented in use over all types of paint and surface. A large compressor (80 p.s.i., 9 c.f.m.) can be used for driving air-power tools. Volume of air : 2–9 c.f.m., pressure of air : 30 p.s.i. (or rather less), up to 100 p.s.i. Weight and cost of plant are high—a minimal compressor delivering only about 2 c.f.m. at 30 p.s.i. will weigh about 40 lb, while a full-scale plant, as described in detail, is heavy enough to run on wheels.

High-pressure spray-painting equipment, capable of doing a fast professional job, consists of a **compressor, receiver, transformer, trolley, air line, paint heater** and **spray gun**. It will spray anything liquid in 10-inch swathes at about 2 miles per hour across the surface, without the need for thinners in paint, so that the paint hits the surface and is instantly dry—without danger of runs or sagging. The paint heater can be dispensed with, and there is a range of smaller compressors, not having air receivers, using smaller guns, without trolleys—the skill needed to avoid runs and sagging increases. This type of plant is certainly capable of a first-class finish, though not with cellulose, which needs to be pushed on quickly.

Detailed description of high-pressure plant

Compressor
A 1-h.p. electric motor (non-sparking) drives the twin-cylinder piston compressor via a V-pulley which is covered with a wire guard (by law). A V-belt will amputate fingers instantly. The compressor gives a constant displacement of about 5·25 c.f.m. at a pressure of about 60 p.s.i. The compressor has an oil bath, which may need topping up once every two years or so with Tapla oil.
    It also has an air intake filter pad, which can be unscrewed from its fitting regularly and soaked in petrol to unclog it.

Receiver
This container, or set of containers, receives the output of the compressor and stores it until needed, increasing the effective capacity of the unit. Must be tested and insured.

Transformer
Compressed air sheds water, and picks up oil, dust and paint. It also arrives at the transformer raw—that is, it is present at the potential of the unit, or rather less when the receiver is emptied, and has 'lumps'—irregularities of pressure and volume from the compressor. The transformer filters out water, which must be drained off at the lower cock, and dirt, which is collected in felt pads. These pads can be replaced at will. It then passes the air to a regulator valve, which allows the pressure to be adjusted up and down. A cylinder pressure gauge is mounted on the receiver or transformer, and an output gauge on the transformer. When the receiver is full at maximum pressure a non-return valve in the compressor output stage triggers an idler device, which unloads the compressor. When air is drawn off through the transformer and the receiver

I

pressure drops, the compressor comes in again. Smaller units may just unload air through a safety valve, larger ones may switch off the motor.

Trolley
Keep the trolley outside the spray booth or area, at the extent of the air-line, to reduce the overspray taken in by the compressor, and to reduce the risk of fire when using cellulose, should the motor burn out.

Paint heater (hot spray cup)
This is a thermostatically controlled heater pot, which contains paint to be sprayed, and which can be fitted directly on to the spray gun, instead of the standard suction cup. It may be used (with great care) with cellulose, where thinners must not be used (by law) in the heater: it is not thought to be very satisfactory for cellulose paints, however, being more useful where using lacquers and oil paints. One of the difficulties is always to get sufficient paint on to the surface to float a high gloss, without having to watch it all run and sag down the work surface a few moments later. Heated paint is thin because it is hot—less thinners are necessary, and the paint therefore has less solvents to evaporate in going off. Hot paint dries very quickly indeed. The paint heater can save on thinners, give a better finish, reduce danger of runs and will reduce overspray by a large factor.

Spray gun
The gun illustrated (fig. 24,1) has an air valve to cut off air when the trigger is released, and draws paint from a 1-quart cup. Smaller guns may take paint by gravity from a smaller cup, or use some of the air pressure to pressurize the suction cup—most smaller guns bleed air when the trigger is released. The suction cup has greater capacity, does not leak paint as gravity cups always must, and is flexible as regards pressure, which the pressurized cup is not. The advantage of not bleeding air is simply that is saves the compressor output and stops dust being blown about when you are between triggered strokes. Small guns have a fixed nozzle, but that illustrated which comes into several sections, is designed to allow any size of fan or cone to be produced, and to be swivelled horizontally or vertically. The adjuster screws are at the rear. Major adjustments involve the changing of the size of the air cap, the material nozzle and the fluid needle: these can be changed in a minute.

It must be emphasized that the gun illustrated has a high consumption, and will not function with less than a 5·25 c.f.m. compressor—but note that, by the time the air has been through all the valves, the receiver, the diaphragm in the transformer, and the air-line, the c.f.m. will be down to 4 (and at least 20 p.s.i. will have been lost). If the gun (or the air cap) is too small, it will tend to inflate. If it is too small, it becomes like firing peas from a howitzer. Perhaps the greatest value in having the larger kind of set-up lies in its flexibility—any kind of work from air-brush painting (Bernard Cohen) to the driving of an orbital sander can be undertaken at a moment's notice.

Usage
Plug the compressor in at the mains with the pressure regulator screw with

drawn, and the drain taps on the receiver and transformer open. Close the drain taps and wait until the compressor is unloaded (receiver is full). Now screw the regulator adjustment in until a reading on the output gauge shows 60 p.s.i., and test the safety valve by lifting it. If there is any air loss at one of the hose connectors it will be audible, and the spanner supplied (all connectors are standard) can be used to make air-tight joints. Half fill the suction cup with water or paint which has been thinned 10% and strained through a stocking, and tighten it on to the gun. Check that the air-hole in the lid is clear, and that the material pipe does not foul the bottom of the cup. Screw in the adjuster knobs at the rear of the gun, and then withdraw the lower one by three turns. Now hold the gun one handspread from a surface, at right-angles to it, and pull the trigger as if to loose three bullets from a machine-gun—pull it *right* back, then let go. The pattern should be conical from the nozzle, and circular on the surface sprayed. If it is not, remove the air cap by unscrewing the holder, spanner off the material nozzle very carefully (so as not to bend the fluid needle), and clean. Replace, checking the seating of the air cap against the gun head before tightening the holder, and check that the packing nut behind the material pipe, through which the fluid needle passes, is fairly tight. If nothing happens again, thin the paint more. If this has already been done, either the transformer is not letting enough air through (needs attention), or the air line is of too small a diameter. $\frac{5}{16}$ inch is standard, not more than 25 feet long. Now trigger the gun again, withdrawing the upper adjusting screw at the rear of the gun. This releases air through two small holes either side of the nozzle in the air cap, progressively pushing the spray into a fan. When the fan control has been withdrawn about four turns, the fan should produce a triggered spray pattern as illustrated. If not, clean the air cap, using a non-ferrous wire or matchstick, or by soaking in acetone, petrol or cellulose thinners. Next check the fan-control adjuster screw—watching from the front as it is withdrawn. The quality of the strained and thinned paint can affect the fan pattern, but not if it is free of nibs, and over-thinned. A weak pattern, or a fan less than 10 inches wide, indicates that you have too large a set-up for the capacity of the compressor: if you have a No. 5 material nozzle, and a No. 8 air cap for instance, try getting the next smaller sizes, or at least at No. 3 air cap, without the two small holes immediately beside the material nozzle in the centre. If you change the material nozzle, you must also change the fluid needle. Note that it is possible to obtain a filter to fit over the material pipe.

Spray with doors open and finished works covered to exclude floating dust—which can get around loose wraps. When using cellulose it is worth while—often vital—to build a duct fitted with an extractor with a rate of extraction (measured in cubic feet per minute) rate calculated to change the air in the spray booth or studio once every two or three minutes. Any likely concentration of petroleum vapours, particularly in the summer, can be ignited by the spark normally found at the light switch for instance. Have an electrician estimate for sealed light fittings, etc. Certain common high-pressure spray problems must be overcome, which are inherent in the system: low-pressure spraying should reduce these hazards to a minimum automatically, though this has yet to be found in general practice.

Overspray: the atomized solvents and excess compressed air produce a mist when spraying, which represents a loss of gloss, paint dust and fire risk. Reduce pressure or reduce proportion of thinners. Do not spray other than at right-angles to the work surface, hold gun one handspread from surface at all times.

Runs and sagging: when the force of gravity overcomes surface tension, the paint sags, then runs down the surface—stipple out flat, rub down. Try again, do not pause while spraying, do not go too slowly, do not use too much thinners, do not hold the gun too close to the surface.

Dry spray: if a gloss paint is sprayed too thick and cannot get through the nozzle it may appear as a mist of dry paint on the surface. This effect is the same as that you get if you starve the gun of paint or air. Thin the paint slightly (this only really applies to cellulose), or obtain more air; increase volume, not pressure. Either a larger diameter air-line, or a shorter one, or a new air filter, or smaller air cap to conserve air. The most common causes of dry spray when using gloss paints (a sandy texture instead of a gloss) is A. the gun is held too far from the work, and B. cellulose paint is sprayed with winter thinners in summer. To correct A., hold at right-angles one handspread from work; B., use a *retarder thinners*.

Orange peel: this is the most common texture. Implies the thinners are not able to float a gloss. Check you are using the right thinners. If you are using cellulose, increase proportion of thinners, shut off draughts, get enough paint on to surface to float gloss. Increase spraying pressure until overspray begins to appear.

Shear: paint 'shear' is caused when pigment or metallic particles separate off from the medium while the gloss is floating. This can mean that the wrong type of thinner is being used, or may indicate that the paint needs more frequent agitation. (See Section Seven Part 2: power-operated paint stirrer). Metallic cellulose lacquers are very prone to shear—do not use cutting paste to rub down final coat.

Bloom: if cellulose paints are applied in a cold studio, or in a draught, a whitish bloom will dull the surface—use *anti-bloom thinners*.

Water: the most common problem. Use a transformer. Replace the transformer felt pads. Regularly drain the taps on the transformer and receiver.

Method

Spray horizontally on vertical surface, pulling trigger fully, and releasing trigger before returning in the opposite direction to overlap first stroke by 50%. Spray horizontal surfaces with strokes parallel to your front, working away from yourself, so that overspray dust does not fall on surface just painted. May be advisable to turn fan 90° and spray vertical strokes if painting a vertical cylinder. Spray edges of box before painting surfaces. Reduce pressure when painting into a corner. Streaks appearing on paint surface indicate that the overlap was insufficient, or not enough paint to float a gloss. Correct tendency to swing gun by turning wrist to maintain right-angled spray at one handspread.

Cleaning the gun

Empty the suction cup of paint, replacing with thinners. Unscrew air-cap holder one turn and spray into a rag until a heavy fog of thinners is atomized. Push the rag over the air cap and spray again—the air will be forced around the loosened fan passages and down into the material pipe to the cup. Repeat with fresh thinners until clean. Remove air cap, material nozzle and fluid needle, clean, oil rear of fluid needle and trigger mechanisms. Refit and blow gun dry with air. Check that packing nut on fluid needle at rear of material pipe is tight. Never soak gun—this rots airtight packings.

Part 3 · Plastics Coatings

In the strictest sense many new paints provide a plastics coating, being based on polymers which harden partly by lengthening of their molecular chains. It is possible to overlay some substances with a thicker coat of plastic material, either by means of dipping, lamination or processes akin to upholstery but using high frequency vibration welding.

See Buyer's Guide for name of firm which will undertake to coat objects with P.V.C. and consult; limitations are imposed by the technology of such firms, which is developing in step with the course of research and the pace of demand.

Laminations fall into two distinct categories: rigid sheet (e.g. Formica and similar sheet plastics) and flexible film (e.g. Fasson). The former is usually characterized by being rather thicker in section, and very rigid, having a lamination of clear plastic over a substrata which has been screen-printed or mass-pigmented. The latter is very thin and flexible. Disadvantage of the former is that it is limited in range by the demands of the interior décor business, and has an edge-section difficult to lose on corners. Disadvantage of the latter is that it may conform to distortions in the surface texture of an unstable (wood or composition) structural material. These materials are supplied with adhesives.

The rigid laminating plastics are made for use with recommended impact adhesives: follow instructions very closely, and note that there can be only one impact—and that it must be in the right place. Supplied up to 10 ft × 4 ft.

The flexible laminating plastics supplied by Fasson (U.K.) Ltd are self-adhesive. Note that some are made for easy removal. Available in sheets, average size 20 inches × 30 inches and rolls 24 inches wide up to any length; it is possible to have sheets supplied to size at special cost. Price varies a great deal between types and properties of material, and on amount purchased. Top price is likely to be charged for small quantity of long-lasting self-adhesive mirror-finish silver, less for a standard size sheet of matt finish black or white. Available in fluorescent, coloured (opaque), gloss, matt and clear finishes, and also in highly reflective form. So far for use only over flat surfaces.

Rigid laminates are ideal for use over chipboard, where edging is possible due to the strength of the laminate. Flexible laminates for use over wood or reinforced plastic or metal or glass surfaces: a matt or gloss paint surface will be excellent as a base for the self-adhesion of this type of plastic.

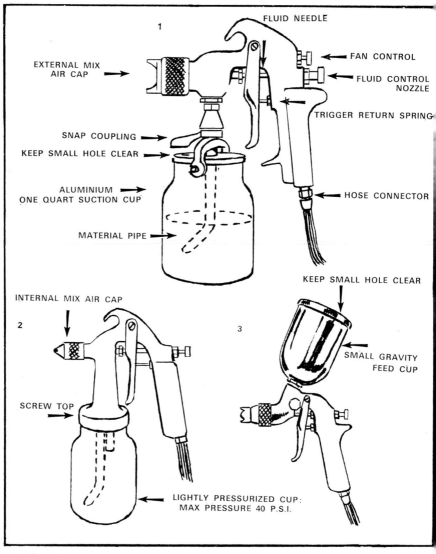

Fig 24

Spray guns
1 High pressure suction feed gun; 60–80 P.S.I. 5–9 C.F.M.
2 Low pressure pressurized cup; 25–40 P.S.I. 2–3 C.F.M.
3 Gravity feed cup for detailed air-brush work.

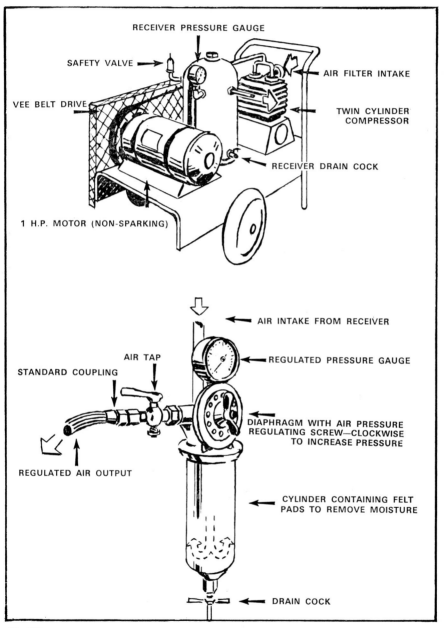

Fig 25

High pressure spray painting compressor and air transformer.
The transformer is usually coupled to a machine like this, which is of the type described in detail in text.

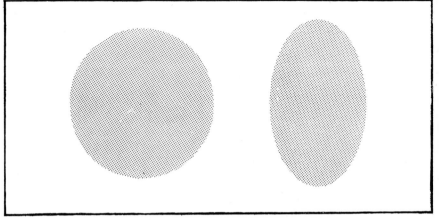

Fig 26

Correct spray patterns: *left*—fan control closed; *right*—open.

U.K. Buyer's Guide to Section Nine (U.S. readers refer to p. 8)

Unless otherwise stated, addresses are London: branches in addition to London are given in brackets.

Pigment and dyestuff manufacturers
>British Titan Prod. Co. Ltd
>Cellon Ltd, Kingston on Thames
>Geigy Ltd
>Pinchin Johnson & Associates Ltd

Synthetic and cellulose paint systems
>Berger, Lewis Ltd. 'Kemitone', etc.
>I.C.I. Ltd. 'Belco' etc.
>Synthetic & Industrial Finishes Ltd
>Valentine's Varnish & Lacquer Co. 'Valrex', etc.

Polyurethane paints
>A. Sanderson & Co., Hull. 'Kingston Diamond'

Oilbound Paints
>Domestic brands, e.g., Valspar, Dulux, Magicote, Starline, Silexine, Celia, etc.

Paint-spraying equipment
>Air Industrial Development Co. Ltd. 'A.I.D.'
>Bink-Bullows Ltd
>Broom & Wade Ltd. 'BEN'
>Burgess Products Ltd
>Aerograph De Vilbis Co. Ltd
>Oscott Equipment Ltd, Birmingham. 'Volumair'

Self-Adhesive plastics coatings
>Fasson (U.K.) Ltd

Protective clothing and equipment—Buyer's Guide to Section Seven

Roy Ascott *Parameter V* 1967
Crylla—stained blockboard $\frac{3}{4}''$ thick, $84'' \times 84''$.
Jig saw and super cutawl shaping, reinforced with
wood framing.
Hamilton Galleries, London *photo: Roy Beston*

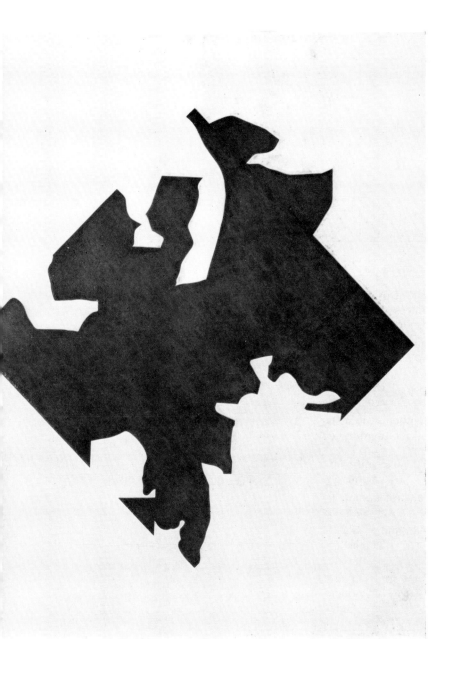

Anthony Benjamin *Carnaby II* 1966
Mass—pigmented polymethyl methacrylate, thermoformed
and reinforced with polyester resins. 6′ × 6′ × 8′.
Photo: Lewis Morley

Tony Delap *Triple Trouble III* (One of two parts) 1966
Wood, glass fibre, reinforced plastic, lacquer.
Robert Elkon Gallery, New York

Anthony Caro *Red Splash* 1966
Steel construction, painted. $45\frac{1}{2}''$ × 69″ × 41″.
Kasmin Ltd, London *photo: John Goldblatt*

John Chamberlain *Shan* 1967
Urethane. 40″ × 45″ × 34″.
Leo Castelli Gallery, New York *photo: Rudolph Burckhardt*

Stroud Cornock *Anthony's Garden* (Relief) 1966
Glass fibre reinforced plastic, extruded P.V.C., cellulose.
19″ × 17″ × 6″
Photo: John Blomfield

Stroud Cornock *Inclining Cross* 1967
Glass fibre reinforced plastic, cellulose. 3′ × 5′ 3″ × 8′ 6″
(extended).
Photo: Tony Allen

Kenneth Snelson *Installation Shot*; (*Audrey II* in background) 1966
Aluminium and steel. 8′ 6″ × 18′ 9″.
Dwan Gallery, New York *photo: John D. Schiss*

Hubert Dalwood *Blue Columns* 1967
Aluminium (brased) and glass. 35″ × 25″.
Gimpel Fils, London *photo: Hugh Gordon*

Donald Judd Untitled, 1965
Galvanized iron. 9″ × 40″ × 31″ each piece ; 9″ between each
piece.
Leo Castelli Gallery, New York *photo: Rudolph Burckhardt*

Geoffrey Clarke *Truni* 1966
16′ high, 3,000 lb. Sand cast aluminium 12% silicon. X.P.
process, cast in four pieces and T.I.G. welded.
Site: New Federal Land Bank, St Paul, Minnesota, U.S.A.
Architects: Bergstedt, Wahlberg and Wold
Art consultant: Duard Laging

Geoffrey Clarke *Plasma Stabile* 1964
10′ high 3,500 lb. Sand cast aluminium—99·5% pure. X.P. process
cast in three pieces, each piece hollow.
Site: United Kingdom Atomic Energy Research Establishment,
Culham, Oxford
Director: John Adams
Architect: Philip Dunthorne

Phillip King *Slant* 1966
Arborite. 84″ × 180″ × 75″.
Rowan Gallery, London *photo: Errol Jackson*

Eduardo Paolozzi *Hagim* 1967
Chrome-plated steel. 2½″ × 11¾″ × 6″.
Hanover Gallery, London *photo: Howards Studio*

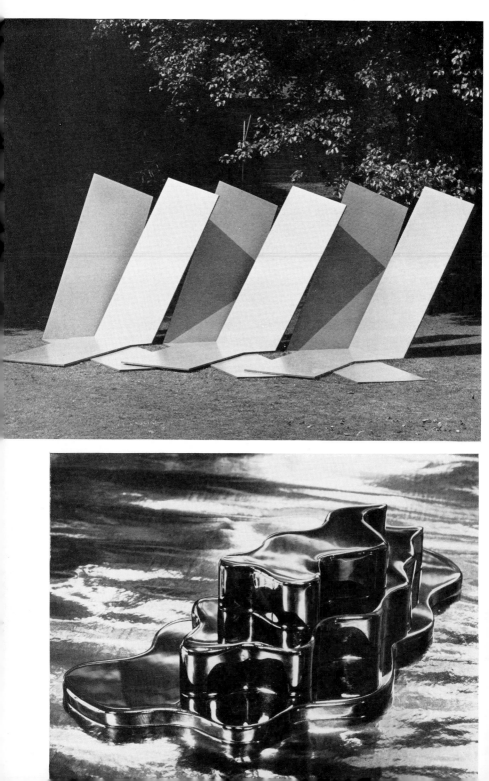

Bryan Kneale *Pressure Point* 1967
Brass, steel, glass. Approx. 15″ high.
Redfern Gallery, London *photo: John Pasmore*

Claes Oldenburg *Soft Washstand* 1965
Vinyl stitched together over kapok, with methacryllic
attachments, all supported over a frame. 55″ × 36″ × 28″.
Robert Fraser Gallery, London *photo: Hans Hammarskiold*

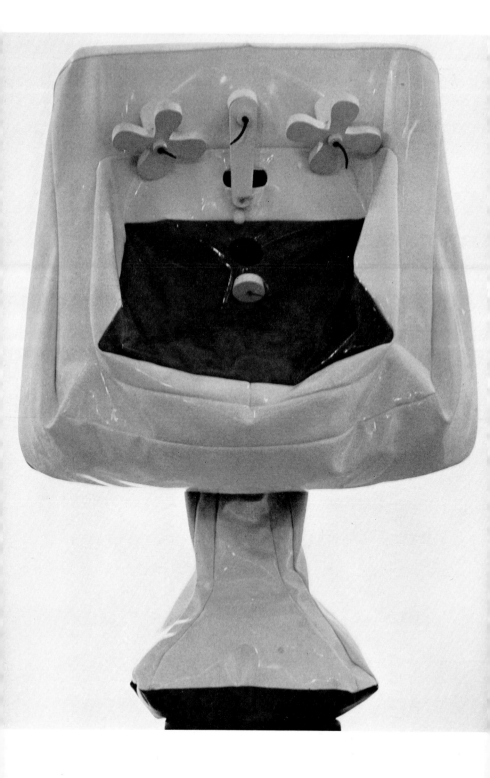

David Smith *Cubi XIX* 1964
Welded and ground stainless steel. $113\frac{1}{8}''$ high.
The Tate Gallery, London

William Turnbull Untitled, 1964
Steel painted silver. 102″ × 30″ × 15″.
Photo: Kim Lim

Robert Smithson *Ziggurat Mirror* 1966
Mirrors. 24″ × 10″ × 5½″.
Dwan Gallery, New York *photo: John D. Schiss*

Derek Woodham *Blue* 1967
Steel painted polyurethane. Cylinders 96″ × 12″, boxes
84″ × 12″ × 6″.
Photo: Errol Jackson

Jean Tinguely *Study no. 2 for an End of the World* 1962
Self-destroying machine complex.
Site : Nevada Desert, near Las Vegas *photo: N.B.C.*

Glossary

A.B.S. Acrylonitrile butadiene styrene copolymer. A dense thermoplastic. P. 121

A/C. Alternating current (U.K. 50~, U.S.A. 60~). P. 54

Accelerator. Substance which increases the rate of a chemical reaction. Pp. 10, 59, 73

Acetone. Inflammable solvent. Strong odour. Chief ingredient of many paint removers. Solvent for synthetic resins. Used to 'degrease' resinous timber. P. 40

Adhesives. P. 102

Adze. Axe-head, where blade runs transverse and not vertical.

Aggregate. Body of pebbles or gravel in cement.

Air brush. Small paint spray.

Air cap. Front nozzle of spray gun having 1, 3, 5, 7 or 9 orifices.

Air drying. Drying without oven stoving.

Alloy. A mixture of metals.

Alum. Double sulphate of aluminium and potassium. P. 16

Alumina. Oxide of aluminium; soft, white, fluffy powder.

Aluminium leaf. Used in **gilding.**

Aluminium stearate. Aluminium-bearing salt of stearic acid. A complex agent widely used to impart thixotropy, stability, flatting and dispersion, and as an extender.

Ampere. Unit of electricity referring to current.

Anneal. To soften metal. P. 50

Anode. Positive pole of an electrical discharge. P. 120

Arc blow. Magnetic distortion of electrical discharge. P. 46

Argon Welding. See **T.I.G.**

Armature. Skeletal support for models. Pp. 10, 111

Amorphous. Indefinite arrangement of atoms; viz. **crystalline.**

Autogeneous. Joined but not **homogeneous.**

B.S.F. British Standard Fine thread.

B.S.W. British Standard Whitworth thread.

Banker. Stonecarving table. P. 88

Bevel. Angle cut off along an edge.

Bituminous paint. Water-repellent, anti-corrosion paints based on asphaltum. See **Brunswick black.**

Bleeder-type spray gun. Where air issued continuously from air cap. P. 130

Blind feeders. P. 28

Bloom and blushing. White crystalline eruption on plaster, cement and other casting materials. White cloud on gloss paint surfaces. Pp. 81, 132

British Standard Specification. Annual directory gives numerical access to standards and measures. P. 52

Brunswick black. Bituminous anti-corrosion paint. Pp. 11, 124

Buffing compound. See **Cutting pastes.**

Butterfly. 'X' suspension support for clay. P. 111

C.C. Cubic centimetre.

C.F.M. Cubic feet per minute.

Cabinet paper. High-grade alumina bonded securely to strong paper.

Calcination. Roasting.

Calender. Machine for rolling sheet plastics.

Cap. Small section of plaster mould through which clay can be removed. P. 13

Capacitor. See **Choke.**

Carburizing flame. Where acetylene exceeds oxygen. Pp. 49, 53

Catalyst. Substance which promotes or increases chemical reaction without itself being affected. Pp. 59, 73

Cathode. Negative pole of an electrical discharge.

Cellulose. Carbohydrate constituent of fibrous vegetation.

Cellulose paint. See **Petroleum Licencing Act.** P. 126

Cement—aluminous. White or black; limestone and bauxite burned together.

Cement—Portland. White or grey, calcinated lime and clay.

Chamfer. A **bevel** edge.

Chasing. Chiselling off burrs on metal castings.

Chipping hammer. Simple all-metal descaling hammer for welders.

Choke. Electrical storage and smoothing capacitor. P. 45

Chopped strand mat. Random glass-fibre sheet. P. 59

Ciment Fondu. See **Cement—aluminous.**

Cire Perdu. The Lost-Wax process.

Clay wash. Separating or release agent for plaster casting—clay + water. P. 14

Cold cure. Without oven treatment.

Colloid. Suspension of particles in gluey substance which is non-crystalline.

Condensation. Moisture shed by atmosphere.

Conduit. Metal sheath for electrical cables. P. 11

Co-polymer. Polymerization where cross-linkage takes place between different types of molecules in plastics terminology.

Core. Substance with which hollow

L

interior of metal casting is filled, e.g. sand or grog, or that hollow interior itself.

Cross-linkage. Lattice joining strands of molecules.

Crystalline. Clear pattern of atoms in a substance; viz. **amorphous.**

Cure. Hardening of a casting material or paint by oxidation or polymerization which may take much longer than hardening (superficial) by evaporation.

Cutting pastes. Abrasive powders carried in a liquid or paste medium used to achieve controlled grinding, polishing, smoothing or buffing of metals, plastics and paints.

D/C. Direct current. P. 54

Degreasing fluid. E.g. trichlorethylene, which removes oil, grease and wax prior to painting, and hot-gas welding.

Dental plaster. Fine white gypsum plaster.

Dermatitis. An allergy causing inflammation of skin following exposure to dust or chemicals.

Dimensional stability. Resistance to warping, shrinkage, expansion.

Dispersion. Mixing or wetting—e.g. action of soap.

Dogs. Iron spikes shaped like a square 'U' which clamp plaster mould sections together.

Driers. Promote paint hardening. Sicatol driers are recommended, e.g. cobalt sicatol. Often poisonous.

Dross. Foreign matter in molten metal. P. 27

Ductile. Capable of being drawn out. E.g. metal from which wire is drawn out.

Dye. Soluble colouring agent. P. 64

Electrode. Point from which an electrical discharge or arc is struck. Often combined with a filler rod to form a consumable electrode. Pp. 51, 52

Electrolyte. Substance between cathode and anode in electrolysis. P. 120

Emulsion. A stable **dispersion** of normally incompatible liquids. P. 124

Esters. Compounds formed where hydrogen is replaced by an ethyl hydrocarbon radical in certain acids.

Exotherm. To give off heat spontaneously, e.g. during **cure.**

Expanded and foam plastics. P. 71

Extenders. Pigments or powders transparent in oil used to give bulk, stability, hardness and thixotropy to paints and resins. Pp. 63, 124

F.R.P. Glass-fibre reinforced synthetic resins. Pp. 100, 112

Feeder. Orifice through which a moulding or casting liquid is to be poured, or cavity which will act as a reservoir where shrinkage is anticipated, e.g. 'blind feeders'. P. 28

Ferrous. Containing iron.

Filler. See **Extenders.**

Filler pastes. Stiff pastes matched in hardness to a material in which it is required to fill cracks, etc.

Filler rod. Rod of similar metal to that being welded (by the T.I.G. process) which does not act as an electrode. Also rod used in welding of plastics.

Fillet. Inset bead of metal.

Flame cleaning. Oxy-acetylene descaling of steel.

Flash. Excess material at seamline o casting.

Flash point. The temperature at which a liquid or its vapours will ignite to a spark.

Flat. To rub down or render matt.

Flour paper. Fine **cabinet paper.**

Flux. Additive which promotes flow and fusion when welding or brasing alloys. Pp 27, 46

French chalk. Hydrated silicate of magnesium. Talcum powder.

Furane. Fine hard varnish.

Gases. P. 52

Gate. Molten metal enters mould through gate via runner from sprue. P. 28

Gel. A jelly substance, e.g. a thixotropic resin, or the phase through which all resins pass in hardening. P. 60

Gilding. Covering with beaten gold, silver or aluminium leaf. P. 119

Glass fibre. P. 59

Glasspaper. Low-grade abrasive; see **Cabinet paper.**

Gold leaf. $3\frac{1}{4}$-inch-square beaten sheets of gold, loose leaf or on waxed paper.

Gold size. Mordant or adhesive to which metal leaves are stuck; see **Japan gold size.**

Gravity feed cup. P. 134

Green. Hardened by evaporation but not cured.

Grog. Heat-porous mixture of ground-fired clay and plaster used as a moulding material in the Lost-Wax or *Cire Perdu* process. P. 29

Gypsum. P. 10

Hardener. See **Catalyst.**

Heartwood. Old inner core of tree-trunk

High polymer. 500 or more linkages between molecular units in a plastic.

Homogeneous. One consistent mass throughout—both in molecular consistency and structural unity.

Hot spray cup. Uses heat rather than volatile solvents to lower the viscosity of paint. P. 130

Hydroscopicity. The property of exchanging moisture.

Inert. Not chemically reactive with other substances.

Inhibitors. *See* **Retarding agents.**

Interface. Conjunction of surfaces, or the space between.

Investment. The clothing of the wax model, runners, etc., with grog in casting by the Lost-Wax method. The grog. P. 31

Isothalic. Of a flexible but cheesy or crumbling consistency. Term for additives which reduce brittleness.

Japan gold size. Fast-drying adhesive used in **gilding.**

Jute. *See* **Scrim.**

Kerosene, Known in Britain as paraffin, which it is not.

Key. Any device used to locate mould parts accurately. P. 93

Key. The abraded surface of a substance for painting.

Kiln. P. 31

Lamination. Building up in layers. P. 103

Lapped edges. Overrunning mould edges when casting in synthetic resin and glass fibre.

Latex. Emulsion or suspension taking the form of a milky liquid. Pp. 17, 94

Lay up. Glass-fibre reinforcing procedure in synthetic resin casting.

Leaching. Removal of soluble elements from a material by light or chemical percolation.

Low energy substances. Lacking frictional characteristics, poor conductors of heat and electricity.

Luminous. Containing crystalline fluorescent pigments, which delay reflection of light by radioactive processes.

M.E.K.P. Methyl ethyl ketone peroxide. A **catalyst** causing **cross-linkage** of polyesters.

M.I.G. Metal inert gas (shielded arc-welding). P. 47

Magazine. A crucible stand used in the furnace. P. 27

Malleable. Condition of metal which allows molecules to rearrange themselves without structural damage.

Masking paste. Whiting, flour, glycerine and glue size, used to mask areas when spray painting. Wash off as soon as paint is dry.

Masking tape. Pressure sensitive crêpe-type adhesive paper used to mask edges when painting.

Mass-pigmentation. Colouring the liquid bulk of a substance.

Matt or **Matte.** Light absorbent surface, or one which disperses reflections.

Medium. The film-forming component of paint.

Melting points. Metals: p. 32. Plastics: p. 72.

Mer. Unit of plastics substance. Complex in itself the mer (monomer, dimer, etc.) is capable of linkage with similar units (polymerization) or different units (co-polymerization) to form long chains.

Methylated spirit. Industrial alcohol.

Microcrystalline wax.

Miscibility. The ability of two or more substances to become homogeneous as a liquid.

Mould. Airborne spores feeding on moist vegetable or animal elements in sculptural materials. Can be discouraged with formalin or alum. P. 16

Mould. Female or negative in casting process.

Neoprene. Synthetic rubber.

Neutral flame. P. 53

Nibs. Foreign particles protruding from paint surface.

Nomograph. P. 73

Non-bleeder gun. Where air issues from the air cap only when trigger is pulled. P. 130

Non-reversible coatings. Where subsequent coats of paint do not soften or affect previous coats.

Ohm. Unit of resistance.

Orange peel. P. 132

Organic. Compounds of carbon (chemistry).

Overspray. P. 132

Oxalic acid. Poisonous bleach for wood, negate with ammonia. P. 119

Oxidation. Effects of atmospheric or chemical reaction where substance combines with oxygen. P 120.

Oxidizing flame. Where oxygen exceeds acetylene. P. 53

P.F. resin. Phenol formaldehyde.

P.S.I. Pounds per square inch pressure.

P.V.A. Polyvinyl acetate. A Thermoplastic.

P.V.A. Polyvinyl alcohol, a release agent, 95% water. P. 61

P.V.C. Polyvinyl chloride. P. 101

Paraffin. Colourless, tasteless, odourless, solid fatty substance. U.K. readers *see* **Kerosene.**

Passivation treatment. P. 120
Pattern. Shape from which casting is to be made.
Patina. Surface produced by ageing or artificially via corrosion, oxidation, polishing or efflorescence. Pp. 59, 81, 121
Peroxides. See **Catalyst.**
Petroleum Licencing Act (U.K.). To have more than 3 gallons of petroleum substance, or to have it in containers larger than one pint—a licence is necessary. Containers must be labelled 'Inflammable petroleum vapours'.
Pickle. An acid or caustic dip.
Piece mould. Plaster mould in small sections from which several casts or slipware items can be removed.
Pigment. An insoluble powder giving colour and opacity. P. 64
Pitching. Bursting off large chunks of stone.
Plastic. Material capable of controlled deformation, e.g. clay.
Plastics. Synthetic (via **synthesis**) substances which can be made to assume and retain a form, either by **thermoforming** or in **thermosetting,** and which exhibit **low energy** characteristics. Pp. 58, 72, 125, 133
Plasticizer. Non-volatile flexible or **isothalic** additive.
P.M.M. Polymethyl methacrylate. P. 70
Pneumatic. Driven by compressed air.
Poise. Unit measure of **thixotropy** or **viscosity.**
Polarization. Arrangement with respect to a field, e.g. +, −, electromagnetic polarity. Pp. 44, 45
Polymerization. The action in which **mers** (e.g. styrene monomer in polyester resin) form linkages in a plastics substance.
Pot life. Useable life of two-pack paints or resins after mixing.
Pressure feed. Where part of the product of a compressor is fed to the paint pot in spray-painting.
Propane gas. Pp. 26, 48, 52, 70
Pyrometer. Ceramic thermometer used in furnaces of kilns, or a thermocouple. P. 27
R.S.J. Heavy steel girder.
Radiation. Heat or light transmitted without affecting an intervening medium.
Rape or **Rapeseed oil.** Used in separating plaster casts from plaster or gelatine moulds. P. 15
Reaction. Action of one chemical on another.

Rectifier. Device which converts A/C to D/C.
Refractory wash. P. 28
Release agent. Any agent which is introduced into or painted on to a mould so as to prevent the casting material later sticking to it. Also known as parting agents, separating agents. P. 14, 61, 81
Relief. Form developed from or into a plane surface.
Retarding agents. Any agent which inhibits an expected chemical reaction; usually the cure or hardening of plaster, resins, cements or paints. P. 10
Reversible coats. Paints which are affected by application of further coats. E.g. the volatile solvents in cellulose paint systems are designed to soften the preceding coat so that three thin coats finish up as one thick one.
Riser. A hole up which molten metal or gelatine finds its level and ejects air. P. 26
Rolling. A method of filling a mould so that there are no seam joints, and which gives a light hollow cast. P. 15
Roman joint. P. 29
Roving. Glass-fibre rope.
Rubbing down. Abrading surfaces to smooth them and/or to form a key for painting. P. 118
Runners. Wax or X.P. connecting rods attached to patterns forming orifices through which molten metal flows from sprue to gate/s. Pp. 29, 30
Runs. P. 132
Rust. Largely electrolytic product of ferrous corrosion.
S.W.G. Standard Wire Gauge. Measure of thickness for metals, e.g. '16 S.W.G.' (approx. $\frac{1}{16}$ inch), which does not correspond to fractional or decimal measurements.
Sagging. Occurs on overloaded paint surface.
Sand-blasting. Cleaning with air-driven shot or non-silica grits.
Sandpaper. See **Glasspaper.**
Sapwood. Soft young outer wood.
Saturated. Complete solution or wetting.
Screed. See **Template.**
Scrim. Open-weave hessian or jute reinforcement material. P. 11
Seam. Joint face on a mould. P. 13
Seasoning. Stabilizing timber by removing moisture. P. 84
Self-etching primer. Contains elements which bite into low-energy surfaces such as aluminium so that the paint will adhere.

Separating agents. *See* **Release agents.**

Sharp sand. Gritty, reflective sand.

Shear. P. 132

Shellac. Brown polish, french polish, button polish, white polish. Natural resin secreted by Indian insects, dissolved in methylated spirits. Pp. 15, 119

Shim. Steel or brass fence used in plaster moulding from clay. P. 13

Silica. Oxide of silicon.

Silicon. A metal. P. 25

Silicone. A polymer of silicon and oxygen.

Silk screen printing. Printing process which has sculptural applications on plastic volumes and sandblasted aluminium. P. 133

Silver leaf. $4\frac{1}{2}$-inch-square beaten silver leaves, used in **gilding.**

Single phase. Electricity supply on one cable, A/C 50~, U.S.A. 60~.

Sinking. Loss of gloss.

Slag. Floating impurities on molten metal, loose slag left in the wake of a welding arc.

Soft soap. A gel used as a release agent. P. 15

Solvent. Volatile content of paints and resins.

Spatula. Wood or metal modelling tool used in sculpture on a small scale; best carved from boxwood, or forged from hexagonal mild steel rod.

Spindle key. The socket spanner which opens gas cylinder valves.

Spray patterns. P. 136

Sprue. The vertical entry cavity for molten metal in founding.

Squeezing. A method of hollow plaster or cement casting where rolling is impractical. P. 15

Stabilizer. An emulsifying agent or a dispersing agent: that is, an agent which keeps paints or resins reasonably mixed up.

Stainless steel. Alloys of nickel, chromium and iron. Three types, varying widely in price according to degree of polish possible, resistance to weld corrosion: Martensitic, Ferritic, Austenitic. P. 100

Stopping. Filling cracks prior to painting wood, etc., or the filler used.

Stoving. Heat fusion of enamels and heat cure of paints and resins.

Striking voltage. Voltage required to initiate an electric arc before **voltage drop.** P. 45

Structural material. One capable of supporting itself with or without reinforcement as a sculptural material.

Synthesis. Union of substances. Union of ideas.

Synthetic paints. P. 125

Synthetic resin. Product of organic chemistry.

T.I.G. Tungsten inert gas (shielded arc-welding). P. 47

Tack rag. Non-drying rag which picks up dust from surface to be painted: recommended.

Tamping. Consolidating. Pp. 25, 81

Temper. The controlled reduction of brittleness of steel achieved by tempering. Pp. 50, 52

Template. Two-dimensional pattern to which a shape can be cut or screeded. P. 11

Tensile. Springy.

Terebine. Strong liquid drier for oilbound paints, which causes discoloration and cracking. *See* **Driers.**

Terracotta. Red clay used for modelling and pottery.

Thermic boring. P. 49

Thermoforming. Heat shaping of thermoplastics. P. 66

Thermoplastics. Plastics in the groups: acetal; acrylic; cellulosic; fluorocarbon; polyamide; polyolefin; styrene; vinyl, which soften when heated, harden when cool.

Thermosets. Plastics in the groups: amino; casein; epoxy; phenolic; polyester; silicone; urethane, which change from a liquid to a gel, and then cure to a rigid material on addition of a suitable catalyst or agent, and do not soften when heated.

Thinners. Volatile solvents.

Thixotropy. From the Greek, meaning 'changing at a touch'—e.g. a gel or jelly which is less viscous when stirred. P. 62

Three-phase. Electricity supply on three cables where the phase of each 50~ A/C current is advanced one-third (U.S. 60~).

Tools. Stonecarving: pp. 82, 87, 88. Woodcarving: pp. 84, 89. General: pp. 103, 113. Power: p. 105.

Tooth. Coarse pigment in paint film which makes it easier to rub down.

Transformer. Pp. 129, 135

U.N.C. Unified Coarse Thread.

U.N.F. Unified Fine Thread.

Undercoat. P. 127

Vacuum forming. P. 67

Vehicle. Liquid component of paint.

Vinyl resins. Pp. 17, 94
Viscosity. Internal resistance to flow of a liquid, measured in Poises.
Volatile. Readily evaporating.
Volt. One ampere of electricity flowing for one second.
Voltage drop. Reduction of **strike voltage** to level suitable for sustained arc-welding. P. 45
Vulcanization. Rubber, etc., sulphurated, heated and so hardened. P. 94
Waste mould. Plaster mould which must be destroyed to reveal casting; much th most common method of getting a re production in plaster from clay model.
Watt. Amperes multiplied by volts to giv electrical consumption or power rating. A 13-amp. power point on a mains voltage o 240 gives a *potential* of 3,120 watts befor the fuse blows.
Welding. Heat fusion.
White spirit. Turpentine substitute.
Wrought iron. Malleable iron.
X.P. Expanded polystyrene. Pp. 18, 26